SCHOOL CHOICE
AROUND THE WORLD

... and the Lessons We Can Learn

EDITED BY PAULINE DIXON AND STEVE HUMBLE

with contributions from

CHRIS COUNIHAN • NICK COWEN
COREY A. DEANGELIS • PAULINE DIXON
STEVE HUMBLE • TRIIN LAURI • KAIRE PÕDER
M. DANISH SHAKEEL • PATRICK J. WOLF • TOBY YOUNG

iea
Institute of
Economic Affairs

First published in Great Britain in 2019 by
The Institute of Economic Affairs
2 Lord North Street
Westminster
London SW1P 3LB
in association with London Publishing Partnership Ltd
www.londonpublishingpartnership.co.uk

The mission of the Institute of Economic Affairs is to improve understanding
of the fundamental institutions of a free society by analysing and expounding
the role of markets in solving economic and social problems.

A CIP catalogue record for this book is available from the British Library.

ISBN 978-0-255-36779-0

Many IEA publications are translated into languages other
than English or are reprinted. Permission to translate or to reprint
should be sought from the Director General at the address above.

Typeset in Kepler by T&T Productions Ltd
www.tandtproductions.com

Printed and bound in Great Britain by Page Bros

CONTENTS

School Choice around the World

Christopher J. Counihan

Christopher Counihan is a Visiting Lecturer and Researcher at Newcastle University and has extensive experience of working on international development and education projects. His primary research interests cover school improvement and pedagogical reforms operating in some of the poorest parts of the world. Dr Counihan has particular interests in peer-cooperative learning and literacy development based on his expertise in holistic child development. He has carried out development research projects in India, Tanzania and Ghana.

Nick Cowen

Nick Cowen is a political scientist with interests in political theory, law and public policy. He wrote his doctoral dissertation at King's College London on the political economy of distributive justice. He has a BA in philosophy from University College London and an MPhil in political theory from the University of Oxford. He became a Fellow at the NYU School of Law in 2018. His contributions to education policy research include *Swedish Lessons, Ready to Read?*

(with Anastasia de Waal) and *Randomized Controlled Trials: How Can We Know 'What Works'?* (with Baljinder Virk, Stella Mascarenhas-Keyes and Nancy Cartwright).

Corey A. DeAngelis

Corey DeAngelis is a policy analyst at the Cato Institute's Center for Educational Freedom. He is a Policy Advisor and Contributing Editor for the Heartland Institute. His research focuses on the effects of educational choice programmes on student achievement and non-academic outcomes such as criminal activity, political and economic freedom, schooling supply, and fiscal impacts. He has published several studies on these programmes with organisations such as the School Choice Demonstration Project, Texas Public Policy Foundation and the Wisconsin Institute for Law and Liberty. Dr DeAngelis gained his PhD from the University of Arkansas.

Pauline Dixon

Pauline Dixon is Professor of International Development and Education at Newcastle University, where she obtained her doctorate. She has been carrying out research into schooling in developing countries for almost twenty years. Professor Dixon has undertaken research projects that include large-scale surveys and census mapping and the testing of children around the world in various subjects, including creativity and motivation. In Delhi her research has examined the teaching of English through phonics and assisting in the implementation, running and testing of an education voucher scheme. Her book *International Aid and Private Schools for the Poor: Smiles, Miracles and Markets* was named one of the top 100 books by the *Times Literary Supplement*. Professor Dixon received a Luminary Award from the Free Market Foundation of South Africa.

Steve Humble

Steve Humble is Head of Education at Newcastle University. He carries out research in sub-Saharan Africa and India on parental choice and schooling. He has expertise in collecting and analysing data from large samples using advanced statistical techniques. His doctorate looked at children's ability, creativity and motivation in poor areas of Kinondoni, Tanzania and investigated the cross-cultural transferability of Renzulli's three-ring concept to an African setting. Dr Humble was awarded an MBE for Services to Education in the Queen's 2016 New Year's Honours List.

Triin Lauri

Triin Lauri is a lecturer in public policy in the school of Governance, Law and Society at Tallinn University and postdoctoral researcher at the University's Centre of Excellence in Interdisciplinary Life-course Studies. Dr Lauri's main research interests are in education policy, school choice and educational inequality.

Kaire Põder

Kaire Põder is Professor of Economics in the Estonian Business School, Talinn. Her research interests cover institutional economics and the economics of education. Her most recent research focuses on inequality mechanisms related to school choice, the ethnic minority achievement gap and school level polices that moderate these inequalities.

M. Danish Shakeel

M. Danish Shakeel has an academic background in physics, mathematics and computer science. His professional background includes software engineering, teaching, education administration and management consultancy. Dr Shakeel was educated in India and the US and he has also worked in both countries. His research interests include religious schooling, school choice, international education, the history and philosophy of education reform and research methods.

Patrick J. Wolf

Patrick J. Wolf is Distinguished Professor of Education Policy and 21st Century Endowed Chair in School Choice at the University of Arkansas in Fayetteville. He received his doctorate in Political Science from Harvard University in 1995 and previously taught at Columbia and Georgetown. Professor Wolf mainly leads or assists with rigorous longitudinal evaluations of private school voucher programs. He has written extensively on school choice, public finance, public management, special education and civic values.

Toby Young

Toby Young is the co-founder of the West London Free School, the first Free School to sign a funding agreement with Michael Gove, and served as the Director of the New Schools Network until 2017. He is the author of four books, the best known of which is *How to Lose Friends & Alienate People* (2001), which was made into a feature film, and three plays. Having worked as a teaching fellow at Harvard and a teaching assistant at Cambridge, he is currently a visiting fellow at the University of Buckingham.

FOREWORD

The Institute of Economic Affairs has a long history of investigating the issue of school choice, and hence of the role of government in education. There have been two basic approaches.

The first has begun with *the fact* of government intervention in education. It has explored ways in which more parental (and student) choice can be introduced into the state system – on the assumption that consumer choice coupled with school competition can raise quality and satisfaction within the constraints of state schooling, as they do in genuinely market-led areas. This was the approach of the IEA's first education monograph, *Education for Democrats* (Peacock and Wiseman 1964), which advocated state-funded education through a mixture of vouchers to parents and bursaries provided by schools, regulated by the state but provided by a mixture of private and state schools. Ideas exploring educational vouchers were continued in later publications in the 1960s and 1970s, to the extent that the erstwhile IEA research director, Arthur Seldon, suggested that all the 'intellectual groundwork' for vouchers had been prepared by the IEA in time for Margaret Thatcher's Conservative government in 1979 (Seldon 1986: 13).

The second approach has been to *question* the role of government in education, and hence to adopt blue-skies thinking about how educational provision for all can best be brought about, with or without the state. This was the approach adopted by E. G. West in his seminal work, *Education and the State* (West [1965], 1994). Here West examined the intellectual justifications for government to be involved in education and found them largely wanting. He pointed to the historical evidence from nineteenth-century England and Wales that showed almost universal schooling provision before the state got involved, and extrapolated from this to suggest only a very minimal role for government in education. This approach has been continued in IEA publications, including some of my own contributions, *Education Without the State* (Tooley 1996), *Government Failure: E. G. West on Education* (Tooley and Stanfield 2003) and most recently *Education, War and Peace* (Tooley and Longfield 2017).

These two approaches clearly bring about different policy prescriptions – and as the IEA publications have featured both the UK and developing countries, there are different policy prescriptions for the UK as well as for international development agencies. The first approach leads to 'top-down' policy prescriptions about how best to bring elements of markets into state education, while the second approach embraces the 'bottom-up' idea that market solutions in education best arise from the spontaneous actions of individual entrepreneurs, outside of any government reforms.

The two approaches, and their different policy prescriptions, are reflected in the essays brought together in this current edited volume, which collates evidence and argument from Europe, North America, sub-Saharan Africa and South Asia.

The first approach is exemplified in Chapters 2, 3, 4, 5, the second part of Chapter 6 and the last part of Chapter 8, where government reforms are outlined that are designed, or appear to be designed, to bring in some aspects of markets – parental choice and school competition – into state educational provision.

Clearly, each of these chapters brings with it some potential policy recommendations. For instance, Toby Young's chapter is supportive of 'Free School' policies, suggesting that they have led to higher educational attainment than the rest of the state sector. Another example is Nick Cowen's chapter on Sweden, which lends support to further exploration of the educational voucher model.

One problem with these approaches is that experience suggests that there is huge resistance to significant reform of existing state education systems. I've mentioned how the IEA got everything ready for the Thatcher government to introduce vouchers in the 1980s – but what happened next brings the sobering realisation that voucher programmes may be a step too far for education's vested interests. Yes, with the 'intellectual groundwork' laid by the IEA, the 'prospect of political action on the voucher quickened' (Seldon 1986: 14). The Secretary of State for Education, Sir Keith Joseph, was convinced by the IEA's work (ibid: 36). A national petition demanding educational vouchers added to their armoury, as the idea went through the government's policy committees. Despite this, at the 1983 Conservative Party Conference, Sir Keith announced that 'the voucher idea was dead' (ibid.: 15). It was dead because the vested interests in education – bureaucrats in the Department of Education, in the local education authorities and the teacher unions – saw no benefit in disrupting the status quo.

So although the evidence from Sweden can be used to point to the success of liberalisation of education under a state-funded and regulated system, this does not mean such a system could necessarily be replicated elsewhere.

The second approach, with its policy ideas of 'bottom-up' private educational provision, is featured in the first part of Chapter 6, Chapter 7 and the majority of Chapter 8. These all focus on the virtues of school choice in genuinely private educational markets.

What are the policy implications from these three chapters? Perhaps, only slightly tongue in cheek, one could say that these chapters suggest that the best education policy is no education policy at all. The evidence given in these chapters (with pointers to a huge body of evidence elsewhere) is quite extraordinary. It appears to show that poor parents in developing countries are not prepared to acquiesce in mediocre government provision, and want control and accountability from their children's schooling. This leads them to use private schools, *even though government provision is typically available at a lower cost* to them than the private schools.

But rather than seeing this grass-roots movement as grounds for celebration, the three chapters also highlight how governments sometimes appear to want to over-regulate this sector. The case of the Right to Education Act in India is a good example. Who can be against the right to education? But the eponymous Act is leading, as the final chapter indicates, to thousands of low-cost private schools being closed in states across India, with hundreds of thousands of children being denied the education their parents have chosen for them.

'School Choice' (with capital letters indicating it is brought about through top-down government reforms) is happening across the world, with varying degrees of success; the chapters in this collection ably examine some of its features and policy implications across the world. But 'school choice' (in lower case, indicating it arises as a spontaneous order) is an extraordinary example of self-organisation. Low-cost private schools emerging to cater for the expressed needs of poor parents provides the strongest case for the virtues of a fully private education system. For me, this is the most inspiring lesson I draw from this collection.

JAMES TOOLEY
Professor of Education Policy at Newcastle University
February 2019

The views expressed in this monograph are, as in all IEA publications, those of the authors and not those of the Institute (which has no corporate view), its managing trustees, Academic Advisory Council members or senior staff. With some exceptions, such as with the publication of lectures, all IEA monographs are blind peer-reviewed by at least two academics or researchers who are experts in the field.

References

Peacock, A. T. and Wiseman, J. (1964) *Education for Democrats: A Study of the Financing of Education in a Free Society.* London: Institute of Economic Affairs.

Seldon, A. (1986) *The Riddle of the Voucher – An Inquiry into the Obstacles of Introducing Choice and Competition in State School.* London: Institute of Economic Affairs.

Tooley, J. (1996) *Education without the State.* London: Institute of Economic Affairs.

Tooley, J. and Longfield, D. (2017) *Education, War and Peace: The Surprising Success of Private Schools in War-Torn Countries.* London: Institute of Economic Affairs.

Tooley, J. and Stanfield, J. (eds) (2003) *Government Failure: E. G. West on Education.* London: Institute of Economic Affairs.

West, E. G. ([1965], 1994) *Education and the State: A Study in Political Economy,* 3rd edn (revised and updated). Indianapolis: Liberty Fund.

SUMMARY

- Education reforms that allow new educational providers to supply schooling into a state system can improve parental satisfaction and raise learning outcomes through consumer choice.
- Private school choice programmes in the US have been shown to strengthen the civic virtues of young citizens. Choice provides children with schooling that matches their interests. A child engaged in school is more likely to learn the civic values being taught and less likely to rebel against social order.
- When the state is unable to supply schooling, as in post-conflict settings where rebuilding to recover from the ravages of war takes precedence, other providers emerge in order to satisfy parental demands and choices.
- Parents from all socioeconomic backgrounds are capable of making informed choices using a range of methods to identify the schooling most appropriate for their children.
- Where government interventions are too rigidly imposed upon policies that target school reform, this can negate the benefits of school choice programmes.

- Unexpected school choice in post-Soviet Estonia offers a glimpse of how historical legacies can mitigate educational inequality.
- School choice can be initiated through top-down government reforms or through bottom-up approaches that are spontaneous and self-organised.
- School choice programmes yield many individual and societal benefits, especially for disadvantaged students.
- Empowering parents through school choice increases parental involvement and produces accountability.
- Education policies need to be informed by gold-standard research to ensure schooling reforms that make a difference to children's lives.

TABLES AND FIGURES

1 INTRODUCTION

Pauline Dixon and Steve Humble

This book sets out to explore school choice in different countries across the globe. In the following seven chapters the authors discuss empirical findings, driven by data, to consider the mechanisms and frameworks that highlight when and how school choice works. Writing about school choice in Europe, America, Asia and Africa allows for a snapshot of where we are currently with arguments, findings and perceptions.

The books starts with a contribution by Toby Young, who assesses the impact of education reforms that have taken place in England since 2006. The focus is on the introduction of Academies and Free Schools. Young also considers the rise in university tuition fees as well as the reforms to the National Curriculum and the public examination system. He concludes that the impact of these reforms has been broadly positive. English schoolchildren have performed better than schoolchildren in other regions of the UK, the number of English children being educated in schools rated Good or Outstanding by Ofsted has risen significantly and the number of disadvantaged English children attending university is higher than it has ever been. When it comes to assessing the effectiveness of Free Schools, Young states that the initial data are encouraging. The attainment of Free School students in Key Stage 1, Key Stage 4 and Key Stage 5 is significantly above average. However, Young believes that more robust research needs to be carried out, suggesting the replication of the lottery-based studies that have been used to measure the effectiveness of Charter Schools in the US.

The chapter that follows by Nick Cowen asks the question: 'Can a welfare-state social democracy deliver choice in education, for all?' From 1992, liberal market reformers in Sweden introduced a general right of families to choose a school and for teachers, religious associations, cooperatives and commercial firms to apply to open new schools. These Free Schools are independently owned and managed but with fees set and paid by the state. This makes Sweden the most prominent example of what is effectively a national school voucher scheme. At the last count, approximately a tenth of primary and secondary school students, and a third of high school students, attended Free Schools.

The best available evidence suggests that the introduction of Free Schools in Sweden has improved educational outcomes, especially in areas where they have managed to open in large numbers. The main mechanism through which they achieved this is raising educational attainment standards in competing state-run schools. However, Cowen believes that the reform has not had sufficient impact to offset other policy changes and social challenges in the Swedish education system. These include a generalised shift towards pedagogical methods that emphasise personalised learning, sometimes at the expense of the acquisition of formal knowledge. There are several ways to account for this somewhat disappointing rate of progress. First, Sweden's regulatory framework may be too rigidly designed to permit sufficient competition. Second, the provision of education itself may face informational asymmetries and externalities that even a fully established market could only imperfectly alleviate. Cowen suggests that the choice of school can only be part of the answer to radical education reform.

Contemporary education philosophers and policy analysts make strong claims that government programmes expanding private school choice undermine civic values and imperil civil society. They argue that democratically controlled government-run public schools are the best vehicle for inculcating civic virtue in the young and that promoting alternatives to the government monopoly provision of K-12 in the US education system threatens the status quo. These claims are testable. DeAngelo and Wolf, in Chapter 4, review the literature that quantifies the effects of private school choice programmes on three important civic outcomes for students in the US: tolerance, civic engagement and social order. Across the eleven empirical studies of the effects of private school choice on civic outcomes, the impacts of choice are neutral to positive for tolerance, neutral to positive for civic engagement, and positive for social order. None of the studies indicate that private school choice negatively affects civic outcomes. DeAngelo and Wolf conclude that, far from being a threat to the civic health of democratic societies, private school choice appears to strengthen the civic virtues of young citizens.

Post-Soviet Estonia, being one of the smallest countries in the European Union, has struggled with problems of social inequality since its transition from communism in the early 1990s. While the indicators of *social* inequality are among the most worrying in Europe, according to the indicators of *educational* equality, Estonia is one of the top performers in the world. Results from the latest PISA (Programme for International Student Assessment) survey indicates that Estonia is among the few countries in the world that succeeds in providing educational efficiency, effectiveness and equity. In Chapter 5, Põder and Lauri explore what role, if any, Estonian school choice policy has had in explaining this unexpected educational outcome. They investigate recent educational policy as well as consider the wider context of the path-dependent historical legacy of Estonia's Soviet past. Relative income equality and a culturally homogeneous population with prevalent secular-rational values characterise this historical legacy. Põder and Lauri build an explorative case study aiming to explain the trajectories of the existent school choice policies and their ability to mitigate any educational inequality.

In Chapter 6 Dixon and Humble consider school choice for the poorest living in Monrovia, Liberia. This has been explored through household surveys and spatial mapping of schools in seven slums across the capital. They also set out the findings from a new government initiative, Partnership Schools for Liberia (PSL), which is the first fee-free national public–private partnership for basic education in Africa. The findings of the spatial mapping in Monrovia reveal a total of 432 schools with only two being run by the government. School types include mission, community, NGO and private proprietor schools.

With the availability of different school management types comes a range of choices for parents. Dixon and Humble go on to look at parental revealed preferences using discrete choice theory. Parents use informal methods to quantify preferences, which are typically informed by environment and context. Focus is often on trust, reputation, caring and commitment in the community itself. One example of this is the finding that parents who state the preference 'safe and close to home' are more likely to send their child to a faith-based mission or community school rather than a government one. Another is where affordability is a preference, then parents are more likely to send their child to a government school. The chapter highlights that poor parents living in a post-conflict situation are able to make choices using a range of methods. It is interesting to note that parents have choices, brought about by the lack of government funding available for schooling after the ravages of war and the most recent Ebola crisis. Only time will tell whether the running of government schools by private contractors will have an effect on school choice as well as learning outcomes and the stability of this west African country.

Critics of school choice make the seemingly rational argument that poverty is correlated with the lack of quality information about products and services. If the argument were true, school choice would lead to the selection of lower quality schools by low-income parents and experimental evaluations of school choice would show consistently negative impacts on outcomes for poor children. Fieldwork would show confused and careless patterns of selection of schools by poor families. In Chapter 7, by reviewing the evidence Shakeel and Wolf dispel the myth that low-income parents cannot choose effective schools. The experimental studies on school choice interventions show that poor families are the main beneficiaries of school choice. Moreover, fieldwork demonstrates that poor parents in developing countries choose fee-paying private schools and reject free government schools. Poverty does not act as a hindrance for poor parents to choose quality schooling for their children. Parents carefully and willingly choose schools of choice for a variety of reasons, ranging from school quality and religious values to safety at school. Academic benefits from parental selections accrue over time. Even for poor, largely uneducated parents, school choice is a journey of empowerment.

The final chapter by Chris Counihan, Chapter 8, concerns the emerging success story of parental school choice in India. Based on recent research, the chapter unpacks critical arguments and recent developments, and charts progression towards a new understanding surrounding choice from recent empirical fieldwork. Encouragingly, parents are seen as 'active choosers' when considering school destinations for their children. This bottom-up movement dispels previous myths surrounding poor parents' inability to make educated choices. The chapter is organised into four sections. First, it considers India's shift towards a liberal economic landscape, which galvanised the education sector based on market-based principles. Second, it investigates parental choice through an ecological lens – offering a theoretical explanation of how various levels of society affect parental choice. Third, there are details on educational vouchers and how these operate in supporting choice. In this section there is a critique of recent evidence on voucher effectiveness on learner achievement. Lastly, the final section concludes by suggesting that there is a real opportunity for international agencies and policymakers to help parents make better-informed choices. School start-ups should be supported and not vilified; they should be allowed to flourish to enable the education market to scale and become more visible. Better-informed parents will facilitate the emergence of higher school quality. In sum, for the Indian schooling system, learner achievement and parental autonomy should be encouraged and facilitated.

2 ENGLISH EDUCATION REFORM: PAST, PRESENT AND FUTURE

Toby Young

The first question anyone trying to measure the impact of the reforms of our modern education system faces is: how far back should you go? The UK's public education system has been in a constant state of flux since the 1944 Education Act. My inclination was to start with Kenneth Baker's introduction of the National Curriculum in 1988, but the difficulty with that is it coincided with the replacement of O-levels and CSEs with GCSEs, so it is hard to compare before and after. More generally, there is a problem with using Key Stage 4[1] examination data as a unit of measurement because the GCSE performance of England's schoolchildren improved year-on-year from the first year they were introduced (1988) until 2012, at which point they stabilised (Figure 1). How do you distinguish grade inflation from real gains?

---

1   School years in England, Wales and Northern Ireland are divided into the Early Years Foundation Stage (4–5), Key Stage 1 (5–7), Key Stage 2 (7–11), Key Stage 3 (11–14), Key Stage 4 (14–16) and Key Stage 5 (16–18).

Figure 1   UK GCSE Level classifications from June 1988 to 2015

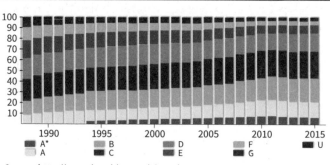

Source: http://www.bstubbs.co.uk/new.htm

PISA

That led me to look at the data gathered by the Programme for International Student Assessment (PISA). The tests it sets for 15-year-old schoolchildren in OECD countries are low stakes and, for that reason, not subject to the same inflationary pressures.[2] But that, too, presented difficulties. UK schoolchildren did surprisingly well relative to those of other countries when they first took the PISA tests in 2000, better than they had done in previous international surveys relative to other nations. However, questions soon arose as to how representative the British

---

2   In fact, the OECD average in maths, science and reading has been declining rather than increasing. The average is set at 500 the first time each subject is the main subject of the survey (reading in 2000, maths in 2003 and science in 2006) and since then the OECD average has fallen. For example, in 2015 the averages for reading, maths and science were 493, 490, and 493 respectively.

participants in the 2000 survey were, with response rates well below the OECD average. PISA included the UK data when it published the results of the 2000 survey, but excluded the UK when it published its 2003 results. UK response rates had not declined further in 2003; they simply failed to improve. But if they were low enough to justify excluding the UK in 2003, why not in 2000? Consequently, I decided to start with the performance of the UK in the 2006 PISA survey, when response rates were in line with the OECD average.[3]

If you compare the performance of English schoolchildren in 2006 with their performance in subsequent PISA surveys (2009, 2012 and 2015) you can get a crude idea of how effective the education reforms introduced by Labour (1997–2010) and continued by the Coalition Government (2010–15) have been. I'm thinking of the policy of converting local authority schools to Academies, which started in 2002, as well as the introduction of Free Schools in 2011.

By that measure, English schoolchildren have shown few signs of improvement since 2006, as can be seen from Figure 2.

That is broadly consistent with other international survey data, such as the Progress in International Reading Survey (PIRLS) and Trends in International Mathematics and Science Survey (TIMSS). Robert Coe, Professor of

---

3   In 2012, the UK Statistics Authority censured the Department for Education and Sir Michael Wilshaw, then the head of Ofsted, for citing the decline in England's standing in the PISA rankings between 2000 and 2009 as evidence that standards had fallen in English schools. The head of the UK Statistics Authority said this comparison was 'statistically problematic'.

Education at Durham University, gave a lecture in 2013 in which he looked at international survey data going back to 1995. He concluded that, while there was some movement among English schoolchildren, both up and down, it was within relatively narrow bands and upward movement in one survey tended to be cancelled out by downward movement in another. '[T]he pattern of results from different international surveys is actually fairly consistent,' he said. 'Not much change between 1995 and 2011.'[4]

Figure 2   England PISA performance

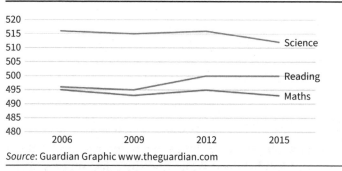

Source: Guardian Graphic www.theguardian.com

However, if you compare the performance of English 15-year-olds in the PISA surveys since 2006 to that of schoolchildren in other regions of the UK, it looks as though they are doing better.

That is a useful comparison because Academies and Free Schools have only been introduced in England, not in the other regions of the UK. Could that be why England was behind Scotland in maths and reading in 2006 but is

---

4   www.cem.org/attachments/publications/ImprovingEducation2013.pdf

now ahead?[5] All four regions have seen their performance in science dip since 2006, but the gradient is shallower for England than for the other three.

Figure 3   School mean GCSE points score in England and Wales over time

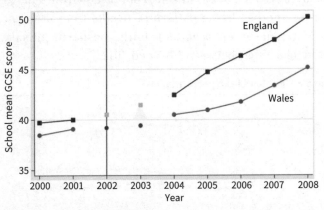

Source: Burgess et al. (2013: 62).

One of the striking things about the UK PISA data is the large gap between Wales and the other regions of the UK, particularly England. That is a relatively recent development and according to a team of researchers at Bristol University is at least partly attributable to the Welsh Government's decision to scrap league tables in 2001, which were first introduced in 1992 (Burgess et al. 2013). In Figure 3, they show the GCSE attainment gap between Wales and England increasing since 2002, when this decision

---

5   The decline of Scottish schoolchildren's performance relative to that of English schoolchildren may paradoxically have been exacerbated by the introduction of the Curriculum for Excellence in Scotland in 2010/11.

took effect. (The vertical line indicates the timing of the policy change, and the two unconnected points are the in-between years, neither wholly before nor wholly after the policy change.)

Academies

Academies are independent, state-funded schools that are funded directly by the Department for Education (DfE) rather than local authorities. They are owned by charitable trusts, which also employ the staff, are not bound by the National Curriculum, can vary the length of the school day, as well as term times, and set their own pay and conditions. The first ones were opened in 2002 by the Labour Government and there were 203 by the time Labour left office in 2010. The Coalition Government then put turbo-boosters under the policy and at the time of writing around three-quarters of England's state-funded secondary schools and around one-quarter of its primaries are Academies – 50.1 per cent of pupils studying in state-funded schools in England are in an Academy or Free School – with the vast majority being 'convertors', i.e. they were previously local authority schools.[6]

A number of studies have been done into the impact of Academies, but most suffer from a lack of methodological robustness. For instance, a PwC report in 2008 found that Academies improved at a faster rate than the national average – but that is not surprising given that the majority

---

6   For a defence of the Academies policy, see O'Shaughnessy (2015).

of Academies set up under Labour were below average performers in their predecessor state (PwC 2008). In what follows, I look at the evidence found by researchers using a more robust approach.

In 2015, a team from the London School of Economics and Political Science looked at the performance of the Academies created by Labour between 2000/01 and 2008/09 (Eyles and Machin 2015). They chose this group because it enabled them to measure pupil attainment before and after the schools converted to Academy status (they only looked at pupils who had been enrolled at the predecessor school). It also meant they could create a control group consisting of pupils at schools that also converted to Academy status with similar pre-conversion characteristics, but which didn't convert until after 2008/09. Using this methodology, they found that the impact of conversion on the performance of the pupils in the treatment group was positive and the longer the pupils had been in the Academies, the better they did, rising to 0.39 of a standard deviation, on average, three years after conversion.

A similar piece of work, using the same methodology, was carried out by another team at the LSE, only this time looking at 205 Academies that opened between 2010/11 and 2013/14, with the control group being 49 schools that converted to Academy status between 2013/14 and 2015/16 (Eyles 2016a). These researchers found that the performance of pupils in the treatment group tended to improve a year before conversion, improved again in the year of conversion, and then began to decline (see Figure 4). Because of methodological uncertainties, it is difficult to draw strong conclusions from this research. In a follow-up piece of work, the same team looked at 1,170 post-2010 convertor Academies and found that where the predecessor school had been ranked 'Outstanding' by Ofsted, the pupils' performance continued to improve with each passing year, but if the predecessor school had been ranked 'Good', 'Satisfactory' or 'Inadequate', conversion resulted in no positive effects.

Figure 4   The effect of post-2010 sponsored Academies on pupil outcomes at Key Stage 4

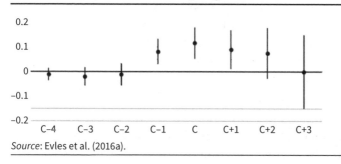

Source: Evles et al. (2016a).

Finally, a piece of research using the same methodology was conducted in 2016 on the impact of Academy conversion on primary schools (Eyles et al. 2016b). The treatment group consisted of primaries that converted between 2010/11 and 2012/13 and the control group schools that converted between 2015/16 and 2016/17.

As before, the only pupils included in the sample were those who had been enrolled at the predecessor schools. The researchers found that, on average, academisation had no impact on pupil performance, negative or positive. That remained true irrespective of the number of years a pupil in the treatment group had been at the Academy and did not vary according to the Ofsted grade of the predecessor school.

These researchers suggest a number of possible explanations as to why the impact of academisation was positive for secondary schools pre-2010, but had zero effect for primaries post-2010. One possibility is that headteacher turnover increased for the first group of schools after conversion, but not for the second. The first group was also more likely to take advantage of Academy freedoms than the second. Another possible reason for the discrepancy is that the secondary Academies in the treatment group had an above-average number of disadvantaged students, whereas the primaries had a below-average number. It could be that academisation is more likely to have a positive effect on the performance of disadvantaged students than non-disadvantaged students. That would tally with much of the research into the impact of Charter Schools in the US (see below). Or it might simply be that the pre-2010 Government gave more money to Academies than the post-2010 Government.[7]

Free Schools

Broadly speaking, a Free School is an Academy created since 2011 where there was no predecessor school. Before 2011, these schools were often called 'sponsored

---

7   Andreas Schleicher, the OECD official who oversees the PISA survey, wrote an article for the BBC in 2015 ('Seven big myths about top-performing school systems') in which he described the idea that there is a direct relationship between the amount a country spends on education per pupil and that country's PISA ranking as a 'myth'. He pointed out that South Korea, the highest-performing OECD country in maths in 2015, spends well below the OECD average per pupil.

Academies', but the range of people and organisations eligible to become Academy sponsors was narrower than those eligible to set up Free Schools and did not include parent groups.[8] At the time of writing, in early 2019, there are 442 open Free Schools, although the number rises to more than 500 if you include Studio Schools and University Technical Colleges.

The Free Schools programme is controversial and a good deal of misinformation about it has been disseminated by its opponents.[9] For instance, it is claimed that Free Schools cater to middle-class families. In fact, there are nearly three times as many Free Schools in England's most deprived areas as there are in the least deprived.[10] Another misconception is that they create places that are surplus to requirements, i.e. in areas where there is no demographic need. But according to the Department for Education, more than 80 per cent of mainstream Free Schools approved to open since 2014 have been in areas where there is a need for additional places (DfE 2017). Finally, it is often asserted that Free Schools are a needlessly expensive way to create new places. However, a National Audit Office report in 2017 found that the cost per square metre

---

8 A group of parents helped set up Lambeth Academy, which opened in 2004, but the school is sponsored by United Learning Trust.

9 Full disclosure: I have co-founded four Free Schools, was a trustee of a Free School multi-academy trust and served as the Director of New Schools Network, a charity that helps groups set up Free Schools, from 2017 to 2018.

10 This figure excludes Studio Schools and University Technical Colleges, which aren't categorised as Free Schools on Edubase, the DfE's register of educational establishments in England and Wales. If you include Studio Schools and University Technical Colleges, the ratio increases.

of building new Free Schools is nearly a third cheaper than the cost of building schools under the last Labour Government's Building Schools for the Future programme.[11] This misinformation is designed to create the impression that Free Schools needlessly take resources away from existing schools, but in reality they are a relatively inexpensive way of creating new school places.

To date, very little research has been done into the impact of Free Schools, partly because many have not been open long enough to have exam results.[12] For those that posted results in 2017 (around 45 per cent), the performance of the pupils as measured by raw attainment varied according to Key Stage. In Key Stage 1 (4–7) they were above average, in Key Stage 2 (7–11) below, in Key Stage 4 (14–16) above and in Key Stage 5 (16–18) above.[13] Pupils between the ages of 11 and 16 also made more progress in Free Schools than in any other type of school in 2017 and 2018. However, these data don't tell us a great deal because we do not know how the pupils at Free Schools would have performed if they had gone to other types of school. In the concluding section of this chapter I argue that more

---

11 'On average, the construction costs of a newly built free school are 29% lower per square metre than schools built under Building Schools for the Future and similar to schools built under the Priority School Building Programme' (National Audit Office 2017: 46).

12 Some research into the impact of open Free Schools on similar, neighbouring schools found evidence of a positive effect, particularly if the neighbouring school in question had below average exam results (see Porter and Simons 2015).

13 These data don't include the exam results for Studio Schools or University Technical Colleges.

research needs to be done into the effectiveness of Free Schools and discuss what form this might take.

Ofsted

At the time of writing, Free Schools are more likely to be rated 'Outstanding' by Ofsted (31 per cent compared to a national average of 21 per cent, although the number falls if you include Studio Schools and University Technical Colleges). They are also marginally more likely to be ranked 'Inadequate'.

Conservative defenders of the post-2010 education reforms often cite the fact that 1.9 million more children are at 'Good' or 'Outstanding' schools today than in 2010, and that is not just because the total number of schoolchildren has increased every year since 2009. In August 2016, 86 per cent of schoolchildren were at 'Good' or 'Outstanding' schools, compared to 66 per cent in August 2010.

But how reliable are the verdicts of Ofsted inspectors? Two pieces of research on Ofsted were published in 2014, one by Policy Exchange (Waldegrave and Simons 2014) the other by Civitas (Peal 2014). Both reports were critical of Ofsted's use of lesson observations to assess 'Quality of Teaching' and both found evidence of a preference on the part of the inspectors for a progressive, child-centred approach rather than a traditional, teacher-led one. Daisy Christodoulou (2014) also found evidence of a progressive bias among Ofsted inspectors. That is cause for some concern, given that the largest and most well-funded piece of research that has ever been carried out into different teaching styles found that the most effective teaching method is Direct Instruction.[14] Nevertheless, Policy Exchange found that there is a strong correlation between the overall Ofsted grade a school receives and the 'Achievement of Pupils' subgrade, with the latter being driven by an analysis of the school's progress and attainment data.

Ofsted is also the chief source of evidence when it comes to measuring behaviour in schools. In 2009, Sir Alan Steer published a report commissioned by the Department for Children, Schools and Families (DCSF) and concluded that overall standards of behaviour were good in English schools and had improved in recent years (Steer 2009). However, his main source was Ofsted, which at that time ranked behaviour 'Good' or 'Outstanding' in the vast majority of English schools. A subsequent report in 2014 by Sir Michael Wilshaw, then the head of Ofsted, said that inspectors had been too generous when it came to judging behaviour in the past and had too often ranked behaviour 'Outstanding' in schools ranked 'Good' overall, or 'Good' in schools ranked 'Requires Improvement' overall, a discrepancy he said Ofsted had begun to address. The report included data from a survey commissioned by YouGov which found that in around 8 per cent of schools 38 days a year of teaching time were being lost because of low-level disruption.[15] In 2016, Tom Bennett published a review

---

14 Project Follow Through, a research study funded by the US Government in which various different teaching methods were compared over several decades.

15 https://www.theguardian.com/teacher-network/teacher-blog/2014/mar/21/michael-wilshaw-ofsted-speech-ascl

of behaviour in schools for the DfE that painted an even bleaker picture. While he acknowledged that there was some evidence teachers thought behaviour had improved since 2008 (from 70 per cent rating it 'good' or 'very good' in 2008 to 77 per cent in 2013; see Table 1), 23 per cent of teachers still thought behaviour was less than good. He concluded that there was a 'national problem with behaviour' in England's schools (Bennett 2017).

Table 1   School behaviour

	2008	2013
Very good	26%	34%
Good	44%	43%
Acceptable	24%	15%
Poor	6%	5%
Very poor	1%	1%
Don't know	0%	<1%
N =	1,442	1,697

Source: NFER Omnibus Surveys.

One reason to be sceptical about the positive tone of Ofsted's assessment of the English public education system is that there is a discrepancy between the percentage of schools being ranked 'Good' or 'Outstanding' and the achievement of England's schoolchildren. In secondary schools, the most important metric by which schools were judged between 2007 and 2015 was the percentage of pupils achieving five GCSEs graded A*–C, including English and Maths (5ACEM). In November 2015, 74 per cent of secondaries were rated 'Good' or 'Outstanding', yet in that year only 56 per cent of all children at England's state-funded schools met this standard. The disconnect is even greater in primary schools. Ofsted rated 84 per cent of primaries 'Good' or 'Outstanding' at the end of 2015 (and at the time of writing that figure stands at 90 per cent), yet according to a piece of research published at the beginning of 2016 43 per cent of children left primary school in 2015 without having achieved an adequate standard in reading, writing and maths (Perera et al. 2016). Having said that, it is possible that Ofsted's judgments are reliable and the reason more children are not meeting basic standards is not the fault of the schools ranked 'Good' or 'Outstanding'.

University access

One piece of positive data is the rise in the number of English students from disadvantaged backgrounds getting into university, which increased every year between 2006 and 2016. According to UCAS, the entry rate for English 18-year-olds living in wards where the level of participation in higher education is in the lowest 20 per cent (POLAR3 quintile 1) was 19.5 per cent in 2016, up from 18.5 per cent in 2015,[16] and 20.2 per cent in 2017.[17] That is the highest percentage ever recorded and higher than for Wales (17.9 per cent), Northern Ireland (16.3 per cent) and Scotland (12.5 per cent). It suggests that the Coalition

---

16 'End of Cycle Report 2016: UCAS Analysis and research', UCAS.

17 'Daily Clearing Analysis: Polar3', 28 days after A level results day, UCAS (https://www.ucas.com/file/125666/download?token=zOWGTXAm).

Government's decision to raise tuition fees did not deter students from low-income families from applying to university. Scottish students do not have to pay tuition fees at Scottish universities and yet a lower percentage of disadvantaged students attend university in Scotland than in any other UK region.

However, these statistics mask a more troubling trend whereby the number of disadvantaged students being admitted to the UK's elite universities as a percentage of the total students admitted is declining. In 2016, the Higher Education Statistics Agency (HESA) published some data revealing that of the 24 universities that comprise the Russell Group, 7 recorded a drop in the percentage of disadvantaged students being admitted in 2015, including Oxford, Cambridge, Durham, Exeter and Imperial College.[18] A report in *The Guardian* in 2013 revealed that Surrey sent almost as many students to Oxford and Cambridge in 2012 as the whole of Wales and the North-East combined.[19] Only 50 students on free school meals were admitted to Oxford and Cambridge in 2014, an increase of just five since 2007.[20] This suggests that the education reforms since 2002 have done little to increase access to Britain's top universities for the most disadvantaged, a conclusion borne out by the Social Mobility Commission's State of the Nation 2016

---

18 https://www.hesa.ac.uk/data-and-analysis/performance-indicators/wi
    dening-participation

19 https://www.theguardian.com/education/2013/jun/09/cambridge-oxford
    -places-south-east, 9 June 2013.

20 https://www.newschoolsnetwork.org/what-are-free-schools/free-school
    -news/poor-pupil-numbers-frozen-in-time-oxbridge-takes-on-just-five

report. Among other things, it found that young people who grow up in poor households are six times less likely to go to Oxford or Cambridge and in 2010 not a single child on free school meals in the North-East got into either university (Social Mobility Commission 2016).

Figure 5   Percentage of pupils taking their GCSEs in 2008 who go on to university at age 18 or 19, by ethnicity and socioeconomic quintile group

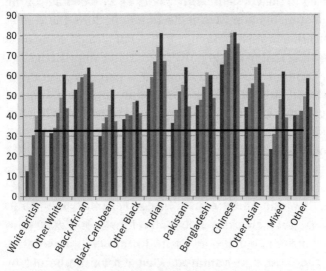

Notes: Bars (from left to right): lowest SES quintile; Q2; middle SES quintile; Q4; highest SES quintile; overall; black horizontal line, white British average.

White working class boys fare particularly badly when it comes to going to university. A 2015 report by the Institute for Fiscal Studies (Crawford and Greaves 2015) found that white British pupils in the lowest socioeconomic quintile are 10 per cent less likely to participate in higher education than any other ethnic group in that quintile (see Figure 5). According to a report published in 2015 by the Equalities and Human Rights Commission, white boys on free school meals are the lowest-achieving group in Britain, with just 28 per cent achieving the 5ACEM benchmark in 2013. That was lower than poor Pakistani boys and poor black Caribbean boys (until recently the worst performers). By contrast, 74 per cent of Chinese boys on free school meals hit that target, and Chinese girls on free school meals were the highest-achieving group in Britain.[21]

Grammar schools

Theresa May's 2016–17 Government announced its intention to open more selective schools in a Green Paper entitled Schools That Work For Everyone (2017), in part as a solution to the problem of underachieving white working-class children. Children on free school meals certainly perform better in selective schools, on average, than they do in non-selective schools, and that remains true if you control for prior attainment. So it is possible that if more highly able, white working-class children were educated at grammar schools they would, overall, perform better (see Figure 6). But the difficulty is that there are not many of these children. At present, roughly half of England's 163 grammar schools give preferential treatment in their admissions arrangements to applicants from disadvantaged backgrounds, yet less than 3 per cent

---

21 https://www.equalityhumanrights.com/en/britain-fairer

of those who get in are on free school meals[22] and very few of them are white British children and even fewer are boys. New selective schools could be encouraged to engage in outreach of various kinds to try to get these numbers up, or the schools could introduce quotas, but they are unlikely to rise by much. One report found that 2.4 per cent of the children being admitted to grammars schools were on free school meals, whereas pupils eligible for free school meals make up around 6 per cent of high-attaining children at Key Stage 2 (Andrews et al. 2016). At present, there are about 500 children eligible for free school meals out of a total of roughly 20,850 in each year group at England's 163 grammars. That would increase to 1,250 per year group if the percentage of high-attaining children on free school meals at grammars reflected the national average.

The main beneficiaries of an increase in grammar school places would likely be the children of middle-class and lower-middle class families, just as they were when grammar schools were expanded in the wake of the 1944 Education Act. According to the 1959 Crowther Report, around 36 per cent of sixth-form pupils at grammar schools were classified as members of the 'professional and managerial' class, 18 per cent as 'clerical', 36 per cent 'skilled manual', 7 per cent 'semi-skilled manual' and 3 per cent as 'unskilled manual'.[23] Moreover, those in the last two categories were unlikely to go to university.

---

22 The overall percentage of children on free school meals in England is 13.2 per cent.

23 The Crowther Report (1959) Ministry of Education (www.educationengland.org.uk/documents/crowther/).

Figure 6 Prevalence of pupil characteristics in the 2016 Key Stage 4 cohort of selective schools

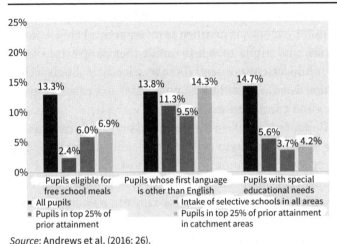

Source: Andrews et al. (2016: 26).

Another report revealed that two-thirds of the children of semi-skilled and unskilled manual workers at grammars left with fewer than two A-levels.[24]

The fact that new selective schools are unlikely to do much to increase the participation in higher education of poor white boys is not, by itself, a reason to oppose them. They may facilitate less dramatic forms of social mobility, from the third socioeconomic quintile to the second, for instance, rather than bottom to top (Burgess et al. 2017). Some teachers at grammar schools praise the hothouse atmosphere of their classrooms, pointing out that it is

24 The Gurney-Dixon Report (1954) Ministry of Education (www.education england.org.uk/documents/gurneydixon/gurneydixon.html).

possible to learn at a faster pace and explore subjects in greater depth, thereby preparing children better for elite universities. Many conservatives believe the expansion of grammar schools is justified from a parental choice point of view and argue that it is unfair that parents of highly able children cannot send them to selective schools if they do not live close enough to one of the 163 existing grammars and cannot afford to go private.

Opponents focus on the supposed harm that more grammar schools will do to children at neighbouring, non-selective schools – by skimming off the most able pupils and the best teachers. But the evidence for this is inconclusive. In 2016 a team of researchers at the Education Policy Institute published a report entitled 'Grammar Schools and Social Mobility' that, among other things, compared the performance of children at non-selective schools in selective areas with that of children at comprehensives in non-selective areas (Andrews et al. 2016). They found that if you define 'selective areas' quite broadly, i.e. allow for the fact that some children travel considerable distances to attend grammar schools, and control for prior attainment, the two groups perform no differently. That suggests that, in aggregate, the presence of a grammar school in an area does not have a harmful effect on children at non-selective schools.

Another group of researchers found that the percentage of all pupils getting 5ACEM in selective areas is slightly higher than it is in non-selective areas (Burgess et al. 2017). However, they did find that children on free school meals performed worse in non-selective schools in selective areas than their counterparts at comprehensives, though this difference was partly attributable to the fact that some of the most able children on free school meals in the selective areas were at grammar schools. Across all state schools, 33.3 per cent of pupils eligible for free school meals got 5ACEM in 2015 compared to 30.1 per cent in selective areas, suggesting that, as things stand, grammars have a small negative effect on the most disadvantaged. The researchers also found that children in the top quartile of the ability range, as measured by prior attainment, performed no better in their 'Best 8' GCSEs at grammars than they did at good comprehensives – and there are five times as many of these high-quality comprehensives as there are grammars.[25] However, they definitely performed worse at poor comprehensives and, by the researchers' definition, the poor outnumbered the good by a ratio of three to one. The Education Policy Institute concluded that more selective schools would neither raise nor lower standards overall.[26]

---

25 That is a slightly misleading statistic in that children at grammar schools, on average, do a larger number of GCSEs than children at comprehensives. So while the average Best 8 point score for children at grammars may be no higher than the average Best 8 point score of highly able children at good comprehensives, their average total point score is higher.

26 Other researchers have found that England's 163 grammars do have a harmful effect on neighbouring schools and that a range of children who attend non-selective schools in selective areas fare worse in their GCSEs than similar children at comprehensives, not just those on free school meals (Atkinson et al, 2006). In addition, various studies have shown that children at non-selective schools in selective areas fare worse by other metrics. For instance, Burgess et al. (2017) found that children with high prior attainment who do not attend grammars in selective areas are 3 per cent less likely to attend university and 8 per cent less likely to go to a high-quality university than similar pupils attending comprehensives in non-selective areas.

The researchers think this is a good argument against the policy. Why bother to create more selective school places if it is not going to bring about any system-wide improvement? But it could just as easily be an argument in favour. After all, if creating more grammar schools will not have any significant negative effects, why not go ahead and do it since it would clearly be popular with many parents?

I feel conflicted on the subject. I went to a grammar school myself – William Ellis in North London, which is now non-selective – and before that I went to two middling comprehensives and failed all my O levels apart from one. Had I not got into William Ellis, I doubt I would have ended up at university. I would not want to deny other children the opportunity I had or one I might easily have chosen for my own children. I am also sympathetic to the argument that if parents of bright children want them to be educated alongside other bright children, and only those children, they should have that opportunity. But I worry that increasing the number of selective schools will lead to a more differentiated curriculum being used across the school system, with fewer children being taught academically challenging subjects and more being steered down vocational pathways at the ages of 11 and 14. I also worry that a great deal of political capital and energy would be needed to create more selective places – it requires an Act of Parliament because it was outlawed by Tony Blair's Government in 1998 – and a government that managed to achieve this might not have a great deal to show for it after five years. With a fair wind, the total number of grammar schools could increase to 200 over a five-year period, assuming few non-selective schools convert. That is still only 200 schools among roughly 24,300 state schools in England – less than 1 per cent of the total. (The total number of state secondary schools in January 2016 was 3,401, so 200 grammars would make up just under 6 per cent of the secondary school total.)

Curriculum and exam reforms

When the first Academies opened in 2002, one of the freedoms they enjoyed was that they did not have to teach the National Curriculum. However, when Ed Balls became the Secretary of State at the DCSF in 2007 he clawed back this freedom, insisting that henceforth any new Academies would have to follow the National Curriculum in the core subjects (English, maths, science and ICT at the time), but not in the foundation subjects (art and design, citizenship, design and technology, geography, history, music, physical education and languages). That curriculum freedom was restored when Michael Gove became Secretary of State at the DfE in 2010, but that did not mean he was indifferent to what was taught in England's classrooms. On the contrary, Gove repeatedly stressed that he wanted all children to study a core of academic subjects and be introduced to 'the best which has been thought and said' (Matthew Arnold's definition of culture). To that end, he oversaw a number of curriculum and exam reforms, including the introduction of a new National Curriculum.

One of the most controversial of Gove's curriculum reforms was the introduction of the English Baccalaureate

(EBacc) in 2011. Initially, all this meant was that a new column was included in the school league tables recording what percentage of children at a school had obtained grade A*–C in their GCSEs in five or more subject categories: English, maths, science, history or geography and a language. This was later expanded to six or more GCSEs drawn from the same five baskets of subjects and then to seven. At present, this is a soft accountability measure, in that schools are not penalised if no children are entered for the EBacc, but it is due to become a hard accountability measure from 2022, when secondary schools will be expected to enter at least 75 per cent of their pupils for the EBacc in Year 10, rising to 90 per cent by 2025.[27] Nevertheless, the percentage of English schoolchildren being entered for – and obtaining – the EBacc steadily increased between 2010 and 2016.

Another reform designed to encourage schools to focus on the academic core was stripping out 'equivalents' – BTECs, City and Guilds, and other vocational qualifications that used to be given the same weight as GCSEs and A levels in the school league tables. In this, Gove was following the recommendations of Alison Wolf, a professor at King's College London who carried out a review of vocational education in England for the DfE and concluded that qualifications in subjects like fish husbandry, nail technology and horse care had little or no labour market value and should not be counted in the

27 This will apply to the vast majority of mainstream secondary schools in England, but there will be some exceptions. For instance, University Technical Schools and Studio Schools will be exempt.

league tables (Wolf 2011). From 2014 onwards, only 70 vocational qualifications were allowed to count as GCSE equivalents in the league tables, compared to over 3,000 before that, and only 400 out of 4,000 were allowed to count as the equivalent of A levels.

Michael Gove also reformed GCSEs and A levels, eliminating modular assessment, decoupling AS levels from A levels and, in the case of GCSEs, banning resits in all subjects apart from English and maths and replacing the old grades with a new grading scale of 1–9. The new GCSEs in English and maths were taken for the first time in 2017, with other subjects following in 2018, 2019 and 2020, while the new A levels were taken in some subjects for the first time in 2017, with the remaining subjects changing in 2018 and 2019.

The new National Curriculum was introduced in 2014 and, in broad terms, differed from the old one in placing more emphasis on knowledge than skills. The programmes of study in English and maths were made more academically rigorous, ICT was replaced by computing and a language was made mandatory in Key Stage 2. It was a much shorter document than the one it replaced, mainly because the old National Curriculum contained a lot of information about 'attainment targets', specifying in great detail exactly what children were expected to know in each different subject as they progressed through eight different 'levels', and included meticulous instructions for teachers on how to assess that progress. The new National Curriculum is less prescriptive, containing next to nothing about 'attainment targets' and nothing about assessment. Gove described it as a 'knowledge-rich, subject specific' curriculum and critics accused him of promoting a return to a Victorian model of teaching in which children were expected to sit in neat rows in front of blackboards repeating facts until they had committed them to memory. In reality, the only thing the new curriculum expects children to learn by rote are times tables – and that was also true of the old curriculum.

In terms of content, the main difference is that the new curriculum supplies teachers with a 'schema' in each subject. That is, they are expected to begin by teaching children some basic factual knowledge, which can then be built upon in a logical, systematic way. In geography, for instance, this means learning the names of the seven continents, the five great oceans, the four points of the compass, the difference between latitude and longitude, the rudiments of map reading, and so on, before going on to tackle topics like sustainability and climate change. Critics of the new curriculum contrasted this knowledge-building approach with a skills-based approach in which children are taught all-purpose abilities such as critical thinking and creativity, but there is little evidence that these higher-order thinking skills can be taught as stand-alone abilities, divorced from subject knowledge, or that teaching children factual knowledge inhibits the emergence of these skills. On the contrary, thirty years of research in cognitive science suggests that children can only begin to think critically and creatively about a particular subject once they have memorised a great many facts about that subject (Willingham 2009).

Following the introduction of the new National Curriculum, various reforms were made to the tasks and tests children were expected to do in primary school, including the introduction of spelling, grammar and punctuation tests in Years 2 and 6. These reforms proved surprisingly controversial – much more so than the new National Curriculum – with parents and teachers claiming that the new, more rigorous testing regime was damaging children's mental health. At the time of writing, no robust evidence has been presented to substantiate this claim.

Many of these curriculum and exam reforms were inspired by the work of E. D. Hirsch, a former professor of education at the University of Virginia who has written a number of books attacking the shibboleths of progressive education and advocating a more traditional approach. What makes Hirsch an unusual exponent of a conservative educational philosophy is that he is a self-proclaimed liberal. Hirsch's main objection to the child-centred, skills-based approach is that it effectively withholds knowledge from children brought up in impoverished, uneducated households, thereby placing them at a disadvantage compared to their more affluent peers, who pick up a good deal of knowledge in the home. 'The unfairness of an anti-bookish ... approach to schooling lies in its assumption that knowledge can be equally withheld from the children of merchants and the children of peasants to achieve the same results,' he writes (Hirsch 1999).

Hirsch has been tireless in his promotion of the knowledge-rich approach and there is some evidence that it is more effective than the educational progressivism that still permeates the public education systems of much of the developed world. For instance, Massachusetts introduced a curriculum much like the new English National Curriculum into its public schools in 1993 and the results were impressive. Scores in the standard tests taken by 10-year-olds and 14-year-olds – the National Assessment of Education Progress (NAEP) – improved and in 2005 Massachusetts children became the first to top the league tables in all four NAEP categories. When the biannual tests were repeated in 2007, Massachusetts topped the table again, as it did in 2009, 2011, 2013 and 2015. In addition, the attainment gap between children from different social and ethnic backgrounds narrowed further in Massachusetts than in any other state between 1998 and 2005 after the new curriculum had been introduced. These effects may not be entirely attributable to the new curriculum – accountability measures changed in the same time period – but they are encouraging nonetheless. 'If you are a disadvantaged parent with a school-age child, Massachusetts is ... the state to move to,' says Hirsch (quoted by Stergio et al. (2012)).

It is too soon to tell whether the curriculum and exam reforms introduced since 2010 have raised attainment in England or narrowed the attainment gap between disadvantaged students and their peers. The first primary school children to be taught the new National Curriculum did not take their Key Stage 2 SATs until the summer of 2017, just as the first students to be taught the new GCSEs and A level courses did not take their first exams until 2017, and then only in a few subjects. The first true assessment will be how well English schoolchildren perform in the PISA tests in

2024, since the 15-year-olds being tested in that year will be the first cohort to have been educated entirely in a reformed system – and that is assuming there is not a resurgence of progressivism in England between now and then.

It is worth noting that there is a tension between the structural reforms initiated by Labour and continued by Michael Gove and his successors and the curriculum and exam reforms introduced since 2010. Both are designed to raise attainment, particularly for disadvantaged children, but the direction of travel in one is towards greater autonomy and diversity, while in the other it is towards more accountability and uniformity. This was particularly apparent in the attitude of Michael Gove towards what is taught in schools, dis-applying the National Curriculum with one hand and steering schools towards teaching a core of academic subjects with the other. This is not altogether surprising and reflects an age-old tension in conservative thought between wanting to roll back the frontiers of the state and, at the same time, not quite trusting people or institutions to behave rationally and intelligently when left to their own devices. However, from the point of view of education researchers this mixed bag of reforms is quite frustrating since it will prove difficult to disentangle the effect of the structural reforms from the curriculum and exam reforms.

Research

While some research has been done into the effectiveness of Academies, very little has been done into the effectiveness of Free Schools. That is because the Free Schools programme is only seven years old and many have not yet posted exam results. However, with each passing year more data are becoming available and it will shortly be possible to do some research. The object should not just be to find out whether Free Schools in aggregate are more or less effective than other types of school. More useful will be to work out which individual schools are the most and least effective. Part of the rationale for the policy was to create a space for innovation in England's public education system so that new educational approaches could be tried and tested. But innovation was never supposed to be an end in itself. Rather, the idea was to discover more effective approaches that can then be replicated, not just by other Free Schools, but by all schools. It is time we assessed those different approaches in more detail.

One useful precedent is the research that has been done into the effectiveness of Charter Schools in the US. Charter Schools are similar to Free Schools and Academies in that they are funded by the taxpayer but are not bound by all the regulations that apply to municipal schools, although they are subject to the same accountability systems and their pupils sit the same tests. In addition, they are set up by parents, teachers and community groups rather than local authorities. The first state to pass a law allowing Charter Schools to be established was Minnesota in 1991 and by 2016 there were around 6,800 charters educating approximately three million children. Unlike Free Schools and Academies, they do not have to be charities, with some states allowing for-profits to own and operate charters. But the vast majority are operated by not-for-profit companies.

Nearly all Charter Schools admit students by lottery, which means researchers are able to measure the effectiveness of charters by comparing the performance of the pupils at the schools with that of the pupils who applied but were unsuccessful in the lotteries. A large number of these lottery-based studies have been done and, broadly speaking, a consensus has emerged: there is little evidence that, on average, attending a Charter School has a positive impact on student achievement. However, there is a good deal of evidence that the average impact of attending a Charter School in an urban area where a majority of the students are disadvantaged, such as New York, Boston or Chicago, is large and positive. As a general rule, these schools increase the test scores of pupils from low-income families when it comes to maths and English by a third of a standard deviation a year, which is sufficient to eliminate the attainment gap between disadvantaged students and their peers after a few years (Hoxby and Rockoff 2004; Hoxby et al. 2009; Abdulkadiroglu et al. 2009; Angrist et al. 2010a,b; Clark et al. 2011).

'No Excuses'

Many of the same researchers have looked at what the most successful urban Charter Schools have in common and, again, there is something approaching a consensus: they are examples of a particular type of Charter School known as 'No Excuses' (Angrist et al. 2010a,b, 2013). This phrase was first used by Abigail and Stephen Thernstrom in a book called *No Excuses: Closing the Racial Gap in Learning* (2001) and has since become part of the *lingua franca* of the American education debate. No Excuses schools typically have the following characteristics: uniforms, strong discipline, high expectations, longer school days, shorter holidays, younger-than-average teachers, regular lesson observations, teacher feedback and an emphasis on the traditional teaching of English and maths.

There is now so much research attesting to the effectiveness of No Excuses Charter Schools, much of it bearing the imprimatur of America's most respected universities, that educators in the mainstream public education system have begun to implement some of the strategies that have proved so successful in the charter sector. For instance, a group of educators in Houston have managed to turn around some low-performing public schools by encouraging them to adopt some No Excuses practices (Fryer 2011). Like the advocates of the Free Schools policy, the pioneers of Charter Schools hoped that creating a space for innovation in America's public education system would enable educators to discover new, more effective teaching methods that other schools could benefit from. And with the No Excuses model spreading across the country, it looks as if that is happening.

To discover which English Free Schools are working best we should use a similarly robust methodology. Some Free Schools select pupils by lottery, while others have a lottery element in their admissions arrangements, and it should be possible to use exactly the same lottery-based method in their cases. Most, however, do not use lotteries, so other methods will have to be employed to create control groups that match the treatment groups. Among schools using straight-line distance in their admissions criteria, for instance, you could create a control group consisting of children who just missed out on places because they live outside the catchment areas. Where that is not possible, you could mine the National Pupil Database to find pupils that match the pupils at the Free School in question when it comes to prior attainment, parental socioeconomic status, special needs, and so on, and create a control group that way. (This method of evaluating schools was used by the DCSF under the last Labour Government and was called contextual value-added.) If a series of studies using these methods is undertaken, and if they are ongoing in nature so they can be refreshed each time Free Schools post exam results, it will not be too long before we discover which the most effective ones are and what characteristics they have in common.

I do not wish to prejudge this research, but it is possible that Free Schools that have adopted an Anglicised version of the No Excuses model will prove to be the most successful. In the Academies sector, some of the highest performing chains are those that, to a greater or lesser degree, have embraced the No Excuses model: Inspiration Trust, ARK Schools and the Harris Federation.[28] We shall have to wait

---

28 These trusts were among the top performers in the Education Policy Institute's first annual survey of multi-academy trusts and local education authorities. In the secondary league table, the Inspiration Trust was the best performer and in the primary league table the Harris Federation came top (see Andrews 2016).

and see whether this is also true of the most effective Free Schools.

References

Abdulkadiroglu, A., Angrist, J., Cohodes, S., Dynarski, S., Fullerton, J., Kane, T. and Pathak, P. (2009) *Informing the Debate: Comparing Boston's Charter, Pilot and Traditional Schools.* Massachusetts: Boston Foundation.

Andrews, J. (2016) *School Performance in Multi-Academy Trusts and Local Authorities – 2015.* London: Education Policy Institute.

Andrews, J., Hutchinson, J. and Johnes, R. (2016) *Grammar Schools and Social Mobility.* Education Policy Institute (https://epi.org.uk/publications-and-research/grammar-schools-social-mobility/).

Angrist, J., Dynarski, S., Kane, T., Pathak, P. and Walters, C. (2010a) Who benefits from KIPP? NBER Working Paper 15740. National Bureau of Economic Research.

Angrist, J., Dynarski, S., Kane, T., Pathak, P. and Walters, C. (2010b) Inputs and impacts in Charter Schools: KIPP Lynn. *American Economic Review: Papers and Proceedings* 100: 1–5.

Angrist, J., Pathak, P. and Walters, C. (2013) Explaining Charter School effectiveness. *American Economic Journal: Applied Economics* 5(4): 1–27.

Atkinson, A., Gregg, P. and McConnell, B. (2006) The results of 11+ selection: an investigation into equity and efficiency of outcomes for pupils in selective LEAs. CMPO DP No. 06/150.

Bennett, T. (2017) *Creating a Culture: How School Leaders Can Optimise Behaviour.* DfE (https://www.gov.uk/government/publications/behaviour-in-schools).

Burgess, S., Crawford, C. and Macmillan, L. (2017) *Assessing the Role of Grammar Schools in Promoting Social Mobility.* London: Department of Quantitative Social Science, UCL Institute of Education.

Burgess, S., Wilson, D. and Worth, J. (2013) A natural experiment in school accountability: the impact of school performance information on pupil progress and sorting. *Journal of Public Economics* 106: 57–67.

Christodoulou, D. (2014) *Seven Myths About Education.* Abingdon, UK and New York: Routledge.

Clark, M., Gleason, P., Tuttle, C. and Silverberg, M. (2011) Do Charter Schools improve student achievement? Evidence from a national randomized study. Working Paper, Mathematica Policy Research.

Crawford, C. and Greaves, E. (2015) *Ethnic Minorities Substantially More Likely to Go to University Than Their White British Peers.* London: Institute for Fiscal Studies.

DfE (2017) More than 130 new free schools to create more good places (https://www.gov.uk/government/news/more-than-1 30-new-free-schools-to-create-more-good-places).

Eyles, A. and Machin, S. (2015) The introduction of Academy schools to England's education. Discussion Paper Series 9276. The Institute for the Study of Labor (IZA), Bonn, Germany.

Eyles, A., Heller-Sahlgren, G., Machin, S., Matteo, S. and Silva, O. (2016a) The impact of post-2010 sponsored Academies, EPI and the LSE (https://epi.org.uk/wp-content/uploads/2016/09/Po st-2010-sponsored-academies-FINAL.pdf).

Eyles, A., Machin, S. and McNally, S. (2016b) Unexpected school reform: academisation of primary schools in England. Discussion Paper 1455. CEP, London School of Economics.

Fryer, R. (2011) Injecting successful Charter School strategies into traditional public schools: early results from an experiment in Houston. NBER Working Paper 17494, National Bureau of Economic Research.

Hirsch, E. D. (1999) *The Schools We Need and Why We Don't Have Them*. New York: Anchor Books.

Hoxby, C. and Rockoff, J. (2004) The impact of Charter Schools on student achievement. Unpublished paper, Department of Economics, Harvard University (https://www0.gsb.columbia .edu/faculty/jrockoff/hoxbyrockoffcharters.pdf).

Hoxby, C. M., Murarka, S. and Kang, J. (2009) How New York City's Charter Schools affect student achievement: August 2009 Report. New York City Charter Schools Evaluation Project, Stanford, CA: NBER.

National Audit Office (2017) Capital funding for schools (https:// www.nao.org.uk/report/capital-funding-for-schools/).

O'Shaughnessy, J. (2015) Academies and chains: when collaboration meets competition. In *Changing Schools: Perspectives on Five Years of Education Reform* (ed. R. Peal). Woodbridge, UK: John Catt Education Ltd.

Peal, R. (2014) *Playing the Game: The Enduring Influence of the Preferred Ofsted Teaching Style*. London: Civitas (http://www .civitas.org.uk/pdf/PlayingtheGame.pdf).

Perera, N., Treadway, M. and Johnes, R. (2016) *Education in England: Progress and Goals*. London: CentreForum.

Porter, N. and Simons, J. (2015) *A Rising Tide: The Competitive Benefits of Free Schools*. London: Policy Exchange (https:// policyexchange.org.uk/publication/a-rising-tide-the-com petitive-benefits-of-free-schools/).

PwC (2008) *Academies Evaluation Fifth Annual Report.* Annesley: DCSF Publications.

Stergio, J., Chieppo, C. and Glass, J. (2012) The Massachusetts Exception.*City Journal* (https://www.city-journal.org/html/massachusetts-exception-13491.html).

Thernstrom, A. and Thernstrom, S. (2003) *No Excuses: Closing the Racial Gap in Learning.* New York: Simon and Schuster.

Waldegrave, H. and Simons, J. (2014) *Watching the Watchmen: The Future of School Inspections in England.* London: Policy Exchange (https://policyexchange.org.uk/wp-content/uploads/2016/09/watching-the-watchmen.pdf).

Willingham, D. T. (2009) *Why Don't Students Like School?* San Francisco: Jossey-Bass.

Wolf, A. (2011) *Review of Vocational Education – The Wolf Report.* London: Department for Education.

3 THE POWERS AND LIMITS OF A NATIONAL SCHOOL VOUCHER SYSTEM: THE CASE OF SWEDEN

Nick Cowen

Twenty-five years ago, Sweden enacted the most ambitious school choice policy seen in the Western world (Klitgaard 2008). On the demand-side, it allowed families to select any school regardless of their residence. On the supply-side, it allowed independent providers to open new Free Schools after satisfying some general regulatory requirements. What particularly caught the imagination of liberal policymakers was that this reform controversially permitted for-profit firms to open schools. This made Sweden, a paragon of social democracy, an unlikely opportunity to test Milton Friedman's (1955, 1997) theory that open competition in education facilitated by state-funded vouchers would better serve the public than monopoly state provision.

Has it worked? The premise of this chapter is that choice has produced observable benefits. It may also have contributed to a few unintended bad social consequences. However, it has not had the impact so far to justify some of the initial excitement. Is this because this reform was not radical enough? Is it because the regulatory framework was inadequate for driving market forces towards better outcomes? Or is it because quality schooling is almost as resistant to market provision as government provision?

This chapter has two fairly distinct sections. The first begins with an overview of the Swedish school system, including the rules and funding arrangements for Free Schools and their expansion to become a major part of the Swedish public education system. Then I summarise the recent academic debate about the consequences of this policy. I note the considerable positive results that school choice has had alongside a word of caution: the results have not been so strong as to overcome other changes in Swedish society and education policy. This means that, overall, results look disappointing. This is a potential warning for school choice advocates in other advanced economies. School choice reforms are generally worthwhile but the resulting improvements may be small at least on formal attainment measures.

In the second section, I depart somewhat from what the academic evidence can tell us in order to explore some of the challenges that these results pose. My argument draws on economic theory and personal experience rather than firm empirical evidence so is discursive rather than probative. I note that the Swedish system has permitted a variety of school types but that the resulting educational approaches have not apparently converged towards systematically better attainment outcomes. This could be because parents lack information about the best schools, because parents have different priorities or because the best schools have incentives not to expand as quickly as competitive firms would in other markets. Further deregulation, including allowing schools to compete on price, may mitigate this concern. But it may turn out that education resists efficient market provision even if market provision remains superior to direct state provision. Finally, I suggest that radical improvements in education may only be possible by departing from our assumption that formal schooling is and always will be central to educational provision.

Overview and history

Before school choice was introduced, local municipalities were almost the sole providers of schooling in Sweden. The exceptions were a few privately funded schools that were out-of-reach of all but the richest Swedes and some foreign residents. In 1992, a centre-right Moderate Party government introduced a general right of firms and associations to apply to open independent free schools, *Friskolor,* and receive public funding for each student who chose to attend. This applied both to compulsory schools at the primary and secondary level and upper-secondary schools (equivalent to sixth form colleges in the UK). In 2006, the reform was extended to pre-schools.

Although the application process to open a new school is slow and demanding, it is systematic in the sense that it restricts the discretion of national state officials. They are not commissioned by the education department in the way that is more familiar with Charter School systems in the US and the Academy system in the UK. By contrast, the application process does allow local public officials to resist the opening of Free Schools. This is arguably the reason that some municipalities – Social Democratic Party strongholds – have far fewer Free Schools than more liberal areas. Nevertheless, this reform effectively introduced a nationwide voucher system.

Funding

The details of funding policy took a few years to settle down. Initially, the value of each voucher was set at 85 per cent of the equivalent of the local municipal schools per-pupil expenditure. *Friskolor* were permitted to charge top-up fees. By 1997, top-up fees were abolished and a principle that parents should not contribute to school costs has remained ever since (Wiborg 2013: 421). While Free Schools are supposed to be funded at parity with local municipal schools, occasionally municipalities have attempted (unlawfully) to subtract a small insurance premium from the voucher on the grounds that the government is still ultimately responsible for providing a school place for every student.

How is the value of each voucher determined? Shortly before the school choice reform was introduced, the national government decentralised funding of schools to local municipalities (West 2017: 69). In a diverse range of countries, including Sweden, England and the US, there has been an increase in the role played by private providers in the delivery of compulsory education (see, for example, Blomqvist 2004; West and Bailey 2013; West and Nikolai 2017; Zimmer et al. 2009). Municipalities can therefore vary expenditure per student in their own publicly managed schools. As a result, Free Schools are funded at parity with students in their local municipal school, not at a national standard. National school chains receive different levels of funding per pupil based on the location of each school. The exception is for Free Schools at the upper-secondary level which offer a particular course that is not offered by the local municipality. In that case, the voucher cost for that course is set by a national list.

This means that while the supply of schools is open to competition and schools accept pupils on a first-come-first-serve basis, willingness to pay is determined collectively through a political and administrative process, whether at a local or national level. This is a market in education of a kind, but one with what amounts to remarkably rigid price controls. Therefore, there is less opportunity for entrepreneurial experimentation that involves varying the price of the service, such as using innovation to drive down costs to families.

Extent

Basic implementation of the reform was a success. Private provision has gone from being a very marginal part of Swedish education to being a substantial feature. In 2005, there were nearly 600 Free Schools at the compulsory level (teaching 74,000 pupils) and over 250 Free Schools at the upper-secondary level (teaching over 45,000 students). In 2013, these had increased to nearly 800 at the compulsory level (126,000 students) and 450 (85,000 students) at the upper-secondary level. That is more than a tenth of compulsory school students and almost a third of upper-secondary students. This is in addition to more than 2,500 pre-school providers looking after around 20 per cent of all pre-school-age children (Skolverket 2014).

It is worth emphasising that the opening of new schools was achieved not through the state subsidising infrastructure for private entities, as is controversially the case for many Academies and Free Schools in England. Instead, the security and predictability of the voucher system was sufficient to draw private investment in to support the opening of new schools and their expansion into school chains. It was therefore the permissibility of commercial education providers with access to private capital that drove much of this growth. While the typical Free School is independent of a large management chain, and there is little evidence of monopoly or oligopoly developing, there are several large popular commercial chains that have driven growth. Non-profit providers are often content with one school.

Moreover, Swedish land-use planning regulation is more flexible than in the UK. This has allowed schools to be established by reconfiguring previously commercial spaces rather than relying exclusively on purpose-built properties.

Academic evidence

School choice has long been a feature of liberal thought. It has traditionally been promoted on the grounds of limiting the state's power to determine children's beliefs and accommodating a pluralism of values, especially religious differences, within a community. However, contemporary support for reforms has been spearheaded by economists who have tended to emphasise the search for the efficient provision of education (Shleifer 1998; Hoxby 2003). This has led proponents to focus on educational attainment, typically established through formal measures such as test scores, as well as cost-effectiveness. Opponents, by contrast, have focused on the issue of social equity in the school system as well as the public value of education that cannot be measured by formal metrics alone.

Free-market proponents theorise the existence of two principal channels through which school choice reforms could improve educational attainment (Sahlgren 2011: 29). The first is the direct impact on students who elect to attend a Free School. Because it is a school of choice, it is hoped to be superior (or at least better matched) to the student than the alternative. The second channel, and more important from a public policy perspective, is a competition effect (Eyles et al. 2016). The entry of new Free Schools into the education market is meant to incentivise improvement in existing municipal schools. This is important because the majority of students remain in municipal schools even with substantial school choice reforms in place. Unless a school choice reform has a systematic effect of this kind, the benefits of choice will always be restricted to the minority which exercise their choice.

The good

Around fifteen years after the reform, promising results from initial economic analyses started to emerge. An increased share of the student population attending Free Schools was associated with moderate improvements in test scores (Björklund 2005; Böhlmark and Lindahl 2007). One particularly promising suggestion was that school choice seemed to benefit children with special educational needs, suggesting that competition encouraged schools to adapt to individual student characteristics more effectively (Ahlin 2003). However, these results were contestable. They were on the margins of statistical significance and their impact was often limited to maths scores, not literacy.

The benefit of another decade has offered stronger evidence for the broader success of school choice (Böhlmark and Lindahl 2015). This extra time has meant that test scores could be validated against educational career measures. This includes the likelihood of students choosing an academic track at the upper-secondary level and continuing education at university (ibid.: 520):

A 10 percentage point increase in the share of independent school students in compulsory school is associated with 1.7 percentile rank higher achievement at the end of compulsory school. Interestingly, the effects also remain positive and significant after compulsory school. A 10 percentage point increase in the share of independent school students increases the fraction with an academic track in high school by 2 percentage points, the mean high school grades with 2 percentile rank, the fraction attending university by almost 2 percentage points, and the average years of schooling by almost 4 weeks. If we convert these estimates to effect sizes, we find that a 10 percentage point increase in the share of independent school students increases both the short-run and long-run outcomes by about 4–5 per cent of a standard deviation.

Another interesting impact of increased independent schools is an observed increase in teacher salaries in both Free Schools and public schools (as well as an increased variation in salaries between teachers). The increase was most prominent among maths and science teachers (Hensvik 2012).

The bad

In contrast to economists, sociologists and researchers in other academic disciplines have tended to be more scep-tical of the benefits of reform. Many have sought to prob-lematise and interrogate school choice as an ideologically driven 'neoliberal' undertaking rather than a reform with a substantial evidence base (Beach and Dovemark 2011; Bu-ras and Apple 2005). Others have pointed to more specific social problems associated with Free Schools. This includes increased segregation by ability, class and ethnicity among students (Öhrn 2011), as well as the additional stresses that a competitive market places on teachers. They also point out that the permissibility of for-profit schools is uniquely unpopular among citizens (Lundahl et al. 2013: 512).

In response to claims that Free Schools have produced better educational outcomes, critics have challenged the reliability of formal measures, arguing that grade inflation has benefited private providers more than the municipal schools (Wikström and Wikström 2005; Hinnerich and Vlachos 2017). They point out the precipitous drop (after the school choice reform) in Sweden's rank according to the OECD's PISA assessment that compares educational attainment across countries (Rönnberg 2015; Lundahl et al. 2013: 508).

The debate

Proponents of school choice have responded by showing that the majority of social consequences attributed to Free Schools are driven by neighbourhood segregation, as well as Sweden's demographic transition from a relatively homogeneous society to one with a substantial degree of ethnic and religious diversity. Rather than the absence of Free Schools in some districts being a sign that the market process drives entrepreneurs to serve only districts with attractive socioeconomic characteristics, proponents argue it is the result of entrenched political opposition by Social Democratic Party–controlled municipalities to new school openings (Sanandaji 2014). Further, they argue that the drop in PISA test scores is a result of a drop in standards throughout the Swedish school system (Böhlmark and Lindahl 2015). Arguably, it is areas where more Free Schools have been able to open that have better withstood this general reduction in school quality.

To sum up, the best attempts to isolate the specific causal impact of school choice suggest that the overall impact on academic outcomes is positive, if unevenly distributed. By contrast, critics of school choice tend to extrapolate from broader correlations and national trends and then impute the worsening outcomes to school choice. Attributing all the problems of a school system that is still substantially state run to the school choice reform seems unwarranted.

Nevertheless, the critique of school choice does have a nasty sting. A reform whose impact can only be discerned after controlling for other social factors cannot be said to be an unparalleled success. It seems that these other factors have overwhelmed much of the impact school choice proponents hoped to see from the reform. In practice, the Swedish system seems to be producing worse educational outcomes compared to twenty years ago. This suggests that a national voucher system alone is insufficient to produce a truly dramatic improvement in education provision.

The limits of choice

Around ten years ago, I and other policy researchers clustered around Westminster's free-market think-tanks were bullish about the prospect of school choice (Cowen 2008). I felt that the then tentative but positive results in Sweden represented compelling evidence for this approach. From my perspective, it seemed that bureaucratic priorities dominated state schooling in the UK. Teachers and school leaders were compelled by government policy to pursue narrowly defined productivity targets determined by the Department for Education and the Treasury. Meanwhile, examination boards were encouraged to make their assessments gameable so that results could be seen to improve continually. None of this ever seemed to relate to the underlying quality of education.

My hope was that school choice would give parents both the incentive and the capacity to identify schools that would best serve their children's long-term interests. The system would become more focused on the local needs of parents, rather than the inspection and examination demands of a state system.

Moreover, with genuine school choice, I imagined schools would be keen to demonstrate their educational quality by selecting credible courses of study and examination assessments. I pointed to the way that one commercial school chain, Internationella Engelska Skolan (IES), had started pursuing internationally recognised English-language qualifications in the form of IGCSEs. This I took to be evidence that schools with autonomy in a competitive environment would be drawn towards widely recognised standards that would also support students entering a global labour market. In other words, a market in education would also support a competitive market in educational standards and accountability.

Far from coming at a cost to teachers' interests, I argued that the autonomy offered by Free Schools would lead to teachers having a more pleasant working environment and opportunities for career development. In the long-term, municipal schools and other Free Schools would have to adopt similar strategies of producing demonstrable benefits and providing an attractive workplace for teachers. Otherwise, they would lose students and teachers to more successful competitors.

Many of the successes that I pointed to in Sweden have indeed been sustained. Moreover, there has been some parallel successes resulting from the introduction of Free Schools in the UK (Adams 2017). However, with the benefit of hindsight and more recent evidence, I now recognise that choice does not inevitably drive towards the best possible outcomes – or at least not towards the aims for which the reforms were publicly justified. There are a number of possible stable outcomes that result from the process of parents choosing a school combined with relatively free entry of suppliers. This process does not always pursue educational attainment as much as policymakers and the general public might wish. There are additional barriers to effective configuration of a school choice framework to produce a substantially higher-quality education compared with the state alternative.

I now explain this problem, as I see it, with an anecdotal example. Then I discuss some economic theories about why this might be so, including imperfect information, differential interests between parents and children, and the potentially large role of signalling in education. I end with some speculative ideas about how this problem might be overcome.

Internationella Engelska Skolan vs. Kunskapsskolan

I think this issue can be illustrated with a contrast between two large and successful school chains: Kunskapsskolan (School of Knowledge) and IES. In 2007, I visited schools at both chains. The school types are very different both in terms of physical architecture, pedagogical approach and

overall educational aims. Kunskapsskolan eschews traditional classroom structures. Their schools contain lots of
variously sized rooms and alcoves designed for personal
study, small-group work and access to new technology. The
students are encouraged to develop and pursue their own
personalised plan in regular consultation with a teacher/
advisor. As a result, they spend less time receiving lessons
from teachers. Students have autonomy to work at school
or at home.

IES, by contrast, uses a more familiar schedule and
classroom format. The schools rely on more teacher-led
instruction and competitive in-class assessment. I found
the ethos to be comparable to an elite independent public
school you might find in the fee-paying sector in the UK.
While IT resources are present on-site, this is not as much
of a selling point as their well-stocked libraries of physical
books. Their main departure from other Free Schools is
their emphasis on English language learning. Their unique
strategy involves teaching English early, then teaching
some subjects (including science) partly in English so that
students become familiar with the subject-specialised vo-
cabulary of the *lingua franca*.

IES make their formal results widely accessible. They
present their results, and compare them against municipal
and other Free Schools, prominently on their website. By
contrast, it is more challenging to find out how Kunskapsskolan fares in formal attainment measures. Of course, even
if comparable outcome data were available, it could always
be argued that any difference in scores reflected the characteristics of their student intake rather than educational

quality. In addition, because the scores are not validated nationally, there are always reasonable ways of contesting comparisons between schools.

There is, nevertheless, suggestive evidence that the learning methods underlying Kunskapsskolan are not as effective as teacher-led alternatives. Attempts to imitate the personalised model in the UK under the Learning Schools Trust brand led to the failed inspections of four Academy schools and their absorption into other Academy trusts (Dickens 2016). There is increasing academic evidence that models of personalised learning fail to measure up in terms of educational attainment compared to more structured teacher-led lessons (Stockard et al. 2018).

In Sweden, however, there are no national examinations and, as a result, inspectors are less able to compare teaching standards. Personalised learning continues to be popular, both among families and policymakers. The market in education has not selected systematically for better techniques and pedagogies. The presence and success of IES suggest that this is not because teacher-led pedagogies are impossible to offer in Sweden. Rather, it is either because the market process has not adequately revealed to families which school types are superior, or because families have deliberately or implicitly chosen schools on the basis of other priorities.

Why does this matter?

IES and Kunskapsskolan are distinctive school offerings. From a purely consumer perspective, this diversity of provision is beneficial. Families have a greater opportunity to select the preferred school ethos and pedagogy for their children. From a family's perspective therefore there is a case for maintaining neutrality between these different school types. The problem is that education is not simply a consumption decision but also a human capital investment decision. Choosing a school that does not emphasise educational attainment may reflect genuinely different family preferences between education, enjoyment and ease. However, for children, who are not in a position to consider their long-term best interests, and for taxpayers, whose interest in education includes maintaining a productive workforce into the future, it is not so clear that a neutral position is justifiable. In other words, there is a potential divergence between:

- the short-term interests of the family;
- the long-term interests of the child;
- the general public's interest in supplying education.

Educational attainment and career success are long-run outcomes. They are also benefits that accrue principally to the child and not to parents. This means that some parents may lack the knowledge and incentive to identify the best available school. There is little prompt or direct feedback for the parents who choose the wrong school. There is not as much opportunity for learning from trial and error as there is in classic consumer markets.

At the same time, there are features of schooling that parents may be tempted to treat as compensating differentials. For example, parents may evaluate the quality of the service according to whether children seem happy at school, whether their peers are considered appropriate and whether the school is easily accessible for a school-run alongside a parent's commute to work. These are all valuable features in their own right but they do not necessarily correlate with educational quality. Even when driven to pursue educational attainment above all other qualities, parents may end up selecting schools with the best student intake as the only observable mark of quality rather than educational quality itself.

Human capital vs. signalling

So far this discussion has assumed that the pursuit of education is both a private and public good. In other words, education is a form of capital that involves deferred enjoyment and effort to obtain in return for greater productivity in the future. Because a better-educated workforce and citizenry benefit all other members of society by making everyone more productive and sociable, it is presumed that education is optimally provided with substantial state support, not just private initiative.

However, other approaches to conceptualising education suggest that at least part of its value in the labour market derives from its role as a signalling mechanism (Altonji and Pierret 1998; Caplan 2018). For example, many of the personal gains from having good school qualifications are not so much the specific skills or expertise taught on the associated course. Instead, people who complete them credibly demonstrate a generic capacity, that they possessed before starting the course, to work reasonably hard on a subject, to defer gratification and to thrive independently in a particular institutional and social environment (that is, among other students at school). It thus signals a capacity that was already within the student, which is very helpful for applying for university or being a credible job candidate. However, the more people who obtain this qualification, the more diminished its power as a signal. This means that in order to possess a more exclusive signal, students may have to go further and acquire a university degree, even though that will not necessarily further enhance their employment-relevant skills.

Signalling, though different from human capital, is still critical for coordinating economic activity. However, the policy problem with education's role as a signalling mechanism is that it is a positional good. It is more characteristically zero-sum when compared with its assumed role in human capital investment. Rather than becoming more skilled and thus increasing the possible range of contributions an individual could make to an economy, signalling is primarily a mechanism for competing and matching for existing jobs (Adnett and Davies 2002). In this sense, policies aimed at increasing 'human capital' could unintentionally contribute, beyond a certain margin, to an arms race to produce what are, principally, private positional goods rather than public goods.

What is the upshot for school choice if signalling turns out to be a significant part of the value of education? If it is, then families may be particularly driven to select the most exclusive school, treating scarcity of available places as the best proxy for quality. Even if they are not treating scarcity as such a proxy, they may find the exclusivity and difficulty of entry itself part of the school's attraction. It would signal how seriously the family takes obtaining education.

Unfortunately, this militates against the profit incentive for successful schools to expand to fulfil demand. For families seeking a credible signal, an expanding school (even of schools with the same brand on different sites) would be less attractive than a school of fixed size with a long waiting list of families that would like to attend. This would explain the comparative lack of overt competition between schools and, conversely, attempts by schools to select their intake rather than appeal to a wide range of students.

Possible ways forward

Both sides of the school choice/monopoly state provision debate have tended to accept that education requires special provision, either because of its nature as a public good or, at least, as a private good for whom the interests of its main beneficiaries (children) require state support and oversight (Ladd 2003). Both sides have tended to accept the moral and practical necessity of making education compulsory and ensuring that children have equal access to a minimum quality of schooling regardless of family resources. This is why school choice reforms seldom permit differential pricing and usually have taxpayers pay the full costs for each pupil.

This does have an impact on the nature of the market. Exit from the compulsory school system tends to be either prohibited by law or prohibitively costly in circumstances where all members of a community are taxed to provide public education. Yet families have different priorities, values and beliefs about schooling. They also have different amounts of time and effort that they are willing to invest in searching for the right school. Without plausible exit options, this may make the market model in education insufficiently competitive to produce socially preferred outcomes.

This suggests that there may be a greater role for government in setting some minimal standards and making sure that some transparent value-added measures of school quality are available to parents (Eyles et al. 2016). If the market alone will not shut down failing schools under the current framework, then a government regulator must have that power instead.

There is a more radical alternative, however. Theoretical developments in political economy increasingly focus on the epistemic, not just incentive, problems with the provision of collective goods like education (Pennington 2014). This perspective brings into question whether there can be said to be one single socially preferred outcome (public good) that can be associated with education. It also encourages us as scholars or policymakers to recognise that even if formal measures of outcomes tend against a particular approach that does not necessarily count against it. Instead, it might be that education has multiple overlapping meanings and functions in a diverse political community. This further calls into question the assumption that most education can or should take place in the form of schooling and whether any system of assessment can adequately evaluate education quality. Pennington (2014: 10–11), for example, argues that there is

> a strong case for leaving the provision, regulation, and funding of educational services to the choices of parents to enter into or exit from relationships with a diversity of suppliers. These may include conventional 'schools' providing a set curriculum on a specialist educational site. Alternatively, they may include a diversity of specialist teachers or institutes providing tuition in a particular subject from which parents select their own customized bundle. Education need not therefore consist of 'school attendance,' but may involve students in a mix of cross-cutting settings including home-schooling, private tuition, membership of civil associations, and employment-based learning.

Thus my more conditional support of competitive markets as simple, demonstrably efficient, solutions to the provision of schooling does not mean I now think an alternative system of monopolistic provision is superior. It does, however, mean that dramatic improvements to the status quo will need a renewed focus on the process through which educational provision becomes competitive. This involves trying to set the right regulatory framework for the existing school system (which may turn out to include proprietary solutions rather than a substantial state role). It also involves permitting greater innovation in ways that may eventually de-centre the role of schools from public educational provision.

References

Adams, R. (2017) Britain's strictest school gets top marks from Ofsted. *The Guardian*, June 16 (http://www.theguardian.com/teacher-network/2017/jun/16/britains-strictest-school-gets-top-marks-from-ofsted).

Adnett, N. and Davies, P. (2002) Education as a positional good: implications for market-based reforms of state schooling. *British Journal of Educational Studies* 50(2): 189–205.

Ahlin, A. (2003) Does school competition matter? Effects of a large-scale school choice reform on student performance. Working Paper, Department of Economics, Uppsala University, Sweden.

Altonji, J. G. and Pierret, C. R. (1998) Employer learning and the signalling value of education. In *Internal Labour Markets, Incentives and Employment* (ed. I. Ohashi and T. Tachibanaki). London: Palgrave Macmillan.

Beach, D. and Dovemark, M. (2011) Twelve years of upper-secondary education in Sweden: the beginnings of a neo-liberal policy hegemony? *Educational Review* 63(3): 313–27.

Björklund, A. (ed.) (2005) *The Market Comes to Education in Sweden: An Evaluation of Sweden's Surprising School Reforms*. New York: Russell Sage Foundation.

Blomqvist, P. (2004) The choice revolution: privatisation of Swedish welfare services in the 1990s. *Social Policy and Administration* 38(2): 139–55.

Böhlmark, A. and Lindahl, M. (2007) The impact of school choice on pupil achievement, segregation and costs: Swedish evidence. Discussion Paper 2786. Bonn, Germany: IZA Institute of Labor Economics.

Böhlmark, A. and Lindahl. M. (2015) Independent schools and long-run educational outcomes: evidence from Sweden's large-scale voucher reform. *Economica* 82(327): 508–51.

Buras, K. L. and Apple, M. W. (2005) School choice, neoliberal promises, and unpromising evidence. *Educational Policy* 19(3): 550–64.

Caplan, B. (2018) *The Case against Education: Why the Education System Is a Waste of Time and Money.* Princeton University Press.

Cowen, N. (2008) *Swedish Lessons: How Schools with More Freedom Can Deliver Better Education.* London: Civitas.

Dickens, J. (2016) An Academy Trust that follows Gove's favourite Swedish model is dissolving.... *Schools Week*, 24 June (http://schoolsweek.co.uk/swedish-company-lets-go-of-its-british-schools/).

Eyles, A., Hupkau, C. and Machin, S. (2016) Academies, Charter and Free Schools: do new school types deliver better outcomes? *Economic Policy* 31(87): 453–501.

Friedman, M. (1955) The role of government in education. In *Economics and the Public Interest* (ed. R. Solo). New Brunswick: Rutgers University Press.

Friedman, M. (1997) Public schools: make them private. *Education Economics* 5(3): 341–44.

Hensvik, L. (2012) Competition, wages and teacher sorting: lessons learned from a voucher reform. *Economic Journal* 122(561): 799–824.

Hinnerich, B. T. and Vlachos, J. (2017) The impact of upper-secondary voucher school attendance on student achievement. swedish evidence using external and internal evaluations. *Labour Economics* 47: 1–14.

Hoxby, C. M. (2003) School choice and school productivity: could school choice be a tide that lifts all boats? In *The Economics of*

School Choice (ed. C. M. Hoxby). A National Bureau of Economic Research Conference Report. University of Chicago Press.

Klitgaard, M. B. (2008) School vouchers and the new politics of the welfare state. *Governance* 21(4): 479–98.

Ladd, H. F. (2003) Comment on Caroline M. Hoxby: school choice and school competition: evidence from the United States. *Swedish Economic Policy Review* 10: 67–76.

Lundahl, L., Arreman, I. E., Holm, A. S. and Lundström, U. (2013) Educational marketization the Swedish way. *Education Inquiry* 4(3): 497–517.

Öhrn, E. (2011) Class and ethnicity at work. Segregation and conflict in a Swedish secondary school. *Education Inquiry* 2(2): 345–57.

Pennington, M. (2014) Against democratic education. *Social Philosophy and Policy* 31(1): 1–35.

Rönnberg, L. (2015) Marketization on export: representations of the Swedish free school model in English media. *European Educational Research Journal* 14(6): 549–65.

Sahlgren, G. H. (2011) Schooling for money: Swedish education reform and the role of the profit motive. *Economic Affairs* 31(3): 28–35.

Sanandaji, T. (2014) Sweden has an education crisis, but it wasn't caused by school choice. *National Review*, 21 July (http://www.nationalreview.com/agenda/383304/sweden-has-education-crisis-it-wasnt-caused-school-choice-tino-sanandaji).

Shleifer, A. (1998) State versus private ownership. *Journal of Economic Perspectives* 12(4): 133–50.

Skolverket (Swedish National Agency for Education) (2014) Private actors in preschools and schools: a mapping of independent education providers and owners in Sweden. Report 410

(https://www.skolverket.se/download/18.6bfaca41169863e6
a65b441/1553965910780/pdf3356.pdf).

Stockard, J., Wood, T. W., Coughlin, C. and Khoury, C. R. (2018)
The effectiveness of direct instruction curricula: a meta-analysis of a half century of research. *Review of Education Research*
88(4): 479–507.

West, A. (2017) Private schools in Sweden: policy development,
inequalities and emerging issues. In *Private Schools and
School Choice in Compulsory Education: Global Change and
National Challenge* (ed. T. Koinzer, R. Nikolai and F. Waldow).
Wiesbaden: Springer Fachmedien Wiesbaden.

West, A. and Bailey, E. (2013) The development of the academies
programme: 'privatising' school-based education in England
1986–2013. *British Journal of Educational Studies* 61(2): 137–59.

West, A. and Nikolai, R. (2017) The expansion of 'private' schools
in England, Sweden and Eastern Germany: a comparative
perspective on policy development, regulation, policy goals
and ideas. *Journal of Comparative Policy Analysis: Research
and Practice* 19(5): 452–69.

Wiborg, S. (2013) Neo-liberalism and universal state education:
the cases of Denmark, Norway and Sweden 1980–2011. *Comparative Education* 49(4): 407–23.

Wikström, C. and Wikström, M. (2005) Grade inflation and
school competition: an empirical analysis based on the Swedish upper secondary schools. *Economics of Education Review*
24(3): 309–22.

Zimmer, R., Gill, B., Booker, K., Lavertu, S., Sass, T. R. and Witte,
J. (2009) Charter Schools in eight states. Rand Education,
California.

4 IMPROVING CIVIL SOCIETY THROUGH PRIVATE SCHOOL CHOICE: A REVIEW OF THE US EVIDENCE

Corey A. DeAngelis and Patrick J. Wolf

Opponents of private school choice claim that a uniform system of public schooling is necessary to teach children various civic values (Durkheim 1956; Apple and Beane 1995; Gutmann 1999; Wolfe 2009). The values often cited as central to the health of self-governing peoples include political tolerance, civic engagement and social order and cohesion (Macedo and Wolf 2004; Wolfe 2009). Without public schools instilling these essential civic values, they argue, democratic societies will not be able to function properly (Saltman 2000; Boyles 2004; Molnar 2013). Early advocates of the common school movement in the US argued that only uniform public schools could teach children common civic and social virtues that would erase or blur sectarian, philosophical or regional differences (Rush 1786; Filler 1983). E. D. Hirsch (2010) also claims that an education system needs to instil a uniform knowledge base in order to create a shared public culture and a functional democracy.

Civic values such as tolerance, respect, order and democratic participation are all important for social cohesion.

What is unclear is whether a single government-run public schooling system is the best mechanism for accomplishing such worthy goals. According to Glenn (1987), the common (i.e. public) school movement of the nineteenth and early twentieth century in the US never succeeded or even sincerely attempted to be an even-handed promoter of a universal pluralistic American creed. The common school movement was about transforming Calvinist farmers and recent Catholic immigrants from Ireland, Italy and Germany into mainline Protestants, as being a mainline Protestant at the time was equated with being 'American' (Glenn 1987: 8). Most public schools in the US taught the King James (Protestant) version of the Bible and recited Protestant prayers throughout the day until the US Supreme Court ruled such practices unconstitutional in *Engel v. Vitale* (1962).[1] The public school system in the US has long been associated with religious, political and social conflict, not cohesion.

Private schools, on the other hand, may have an advantage in inculcating these values to children in the US and elsewhere. Private schools have an incentive to cater to the needs of individual families, and parents value the citizenship skills of their children (Friedman and Friedman 1990; Neal 2002; Witte 2004). Private school choice allows for an improved match between the interests of children and educators, which increases the likelihood that children will be engaged at school. If children are more engaged in school, they will be more likely to learn the civic values

---

1 *Engel v. Vitale [1962]* 370 (US), p. 421.

being taught, and less likely to feel rebellious against social order.

Perhaps most importantly, since public schools explicitly aim to instil a uniform set of values and ideas, a system of private schooling may increase the likelihood that students will confront alternative viewpoints and engage in meaningful discussion of contentious issues with both their teachers and their peers. Essential debates and dialogue may be less likely to take place in public schools, so private schools may be better equipped to diminish intolerance between people holding competing views. Evidence that private schools are more effective at teaching democratic values could be a vital reason to expand private school choice programmes in the US.

Most evaluations of private school choice focus on student achievement as measured by standardised test scores. Around the world, experimental evidence indicates that additional options generated through private school choice programmes produce slightly higher student achievement (Shakeel et al. 2016). Only two recent experimental evaluations of private school choice show negative impacts on student achievement in their final study year, one of the Louisiana Scholarship Program (Abdulkadiroglu et al. 2015) and one of the Opportunity Scholarship Program in Washington, DC (Dynarski et al. 2017). Notably, a second experimental evaluation of the Louisiana programme finds that children in private schools catch up to their control group counterparts in student achievement after three years in the programme (Mills and Wolf 2017).

While the impacts have been generally small and positive for student test scores, all of the research on student educational attainment has found large positive impacts of private schooling on high school graduation, college enrolment and college completion rates (Neal 1997; Warren 2008; Cowen et al. 2013; Wolf et al. 2013). In particular, Cowen et al. (2013) found that the Milwaukee Parental Choice Program (MPCP) improved graduation rates by seven percentage points and Wolf et al. (2013) found that the DC Opportunity Scholarship Program (OSP) improved graduation rates by over twenty percentage points. Private schools may be most beneficial through improving non-cognitive skills of students such as motivation and determination more closely related to civic outcomes than to test scores.

While these results are clearly positive for private school choice, such programmes enrol less than 1 per cent of the students in the US. Generalising these outcomes to the rest of the student population must be accompanied with caution. Theoretically, since most private school choice programmes in the US are targeted to the least-advantaged children in society, the effects could be smaller, or even negative, for more-advantaged groups of students. Alternatively, impacts on students and society could be much more positive if competition from expanded school choice improves the general supply of education in the US. If private schools can shape non-cognitive skills and graduation rates, they may also be able to shape character and citizenship skills that are valuable to society as a whole. However, the theoretical arguments surrounding private schooling and citizenship skills are complex and compelling on both sides, so it is necessary to examine the existing empirical evidence.

In this chapter, we examine the effects of private school choice programmes on tolerance, civic engagement and social order for students in the US. For tolerance, we review studies that examine any type of tolerance of others as an outcome measure. For civic engagement, we include studies of voting behaviour, charitable giving and volunteering. For social order, we examine studies of criminal activity.

Theory

We are familiar with three general theories for how school choice could benefit society. The first two theories are grounded in basic economic principles. The current system of schooling allows public schools to have a monopoly on public funding, which ultimately leads to them wielding monopoly power. Monopoly power generally leads to lower quality service at a higher price (Smith 1776). Since public schools have a monopoly on public funding, they do not face a substantial threat of competition from private schools. Consequently, they may not have a sufficient incentive to improve quality or decrease expenses (Hoxby 2007; Chubb and Moe 2011). They may even have an incentive to increase expenditures each year rather than become more efficient (Niskanen 1971).

A second potential economic benefit of school choice, alongside competitive pressures to increase quality is specialisation. School choice programmes can improve the match between school and student. This allocative efficiency is particularly important in the education sector since all children are unique; they have diverse interests, learning abilities and learning styles (Viteritti et al. 2005: 167). The increase in quality in schooling due to a better parental match of child to school could improve student test scores as well as citizenship skills.

Thirdly, since a system of private schooling decreases the monopoly that public institutions have on information and the standardisation of educational delivery, private school choice could increase the likelihood that a student encounters alternative viewpoints within their school and in society. This increased exposure to differing points of view could lead individual students to become more respectful, accepting and knowledgeable about the arguments of other groups (Short 2002). Students and educators in private schools may be more open about discussing topics that would appear controversial in the public sphere. Since selection into and out of private schools is voluntary, and based on interests more so than neighbourhood, students may feel more encouraged to discuss alternative viewpoints. On the other hand, students in a public setting may be more likely to fear insulting or offending other groups of students, therefore discussions of controversial issues may not happen at all (Berkman and Plutzer 2010). When argumentative exchanges do not occur during the formative period of a student's life, they are less likely to recognise and tolerate the views of groups with whom they disagree when they encounter them later in life.

Lastly, school choice is more pluralistic than a government monopoly on schooling and can lead to a dispersion and balance of power within the realm of education (Galston 2004). A private school choice programme reduces the monopoly that public schools and their leaders currently hold on power by shifting authority to families. The resulting balance of power could lead to citizens feeling more in control of their own lives (Stewart and Wolf 2014). The feeling of control and autonomy could reduce the likelihood that citizens will engage in rebellious behaviour such as breaking implicit or explicit laws in society (Figure 7). While this specific theory has not been tested empirically, there is significant evidence that autonomy leads to increased satisfaction and decreased stress (Finn 2001). Greater levels of happiness and lower levels of stress lead to less irrational behaviours such as criminal activity and a lack of respect for others (Artello and Williams 2014).

There also are strong theoretical arguments that lead to a less-optimistic conclusion: that private school choice could harm society. Theoretically, if school quality includes the ability of schools to alter civic behaviour, and private schools are of lower quality than publicly run schools, then private school choice could harm civic outcomes.

Critics of private schooling argue that since individuals are self-interested, they will not demand the type of schooling that improves social outcomes. Moreover, individuals exercising private school choice may self-select into environments that reinforce their pre-existing interests and biases against other groups of people (Cheng and DeLany 1999; Ladd 2002; Mathews 2006).

Figure 7   How school choice influences civic values

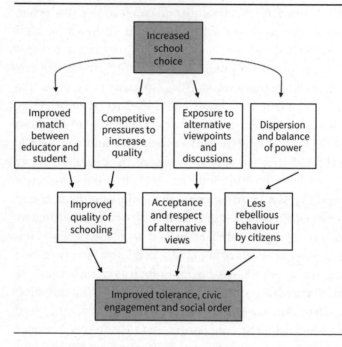

Perhaps most prominent is the historical argument that public schools are necessary for a stable democratic society since they force children from diverse backgrounds to spend time with one another. If children from a wide array of backgrounds, religions and races are in the same classroom, they may become more accepting of each other since they would have the opportunity to discuss opposing views (Filler 1983). In addition, government-run schools may have a strong interest in inculcating character skills, the benefits of which accrue to third parties.

Since there may be equally compelling theoretical arguments on either side of the question of the civic effects of private school choice, a review of the empirical evidence is necessary.

Review content

We conducted a systematic search of the published academic and research literature on school choice to identify studies of choice and civic values. We supplemented that search with information from our own networks. In our review of the evidence, we found eleven evaluations of private school choice programmes in the US that focused on civic outcomes. The evaluations took place in Washington, DC (two studies), Milwaukee (four studies), Louisiana (one study), New York City (one study), and across the country via the privately funded Children's Scholarship Fund (three studies). In our review of these studies, we call special attention to the most rigorous analyses that use random assignment experimental techniques. Six of these evaluations examined tolerance as an outcome measure.

Tolerance

The evaluations of private school choice programmes in DC, Louisiana and nationwide through the Children's Scholarship Fund (CSF) were all experimental randomised field trials. Three out of five of these analyses did not detect any effect of private school choice on tolerance of others (Table 2). Two experimental evaluations, one of the DC programme and one of the CSF, found positive impacts of private school vouchers on tolerance of others (Wolf et al. 2001; Campbell 2002). Based on responses to three survey questions about tolerance of others, Wolf et al. (2001) found that winning a private school voucher lottery increased tolerance levels between 6.7 and 8.2 percentage points. Actually attending a private school in DC increased tolerance levels by between 16.4 and 20.2 percentage points. David Campbell (2002) found that switching from a public to a private school via the CSF programme increased students' political tolerance index score by 0.8 points, which represented more than one standard deviation increase in tolerance.

Table 2   The effect of school choice on tolerance

Study	Programme	Design	Finding
Campbell (2002)	CSF	RFT	+
Howell and Peterson (2006)	DC OSP	RFT	Null
Mills et al. (2016)	LSP	RFT	Null
Peterson and Campbell (2001)	CSF	RFT	Null
Wolf et al. (2001)	DC OSP	RFT	+
Fleming et al. (2014)	MPCP	Matching QED	+

Note: Null indicates that the study did not detect any statistically significant effect on tolerance of others. A box highlighted in grey indicates that the study found statistically significant positive effects on tolerance of others.

The only non-experimental study of the effect of private schooling on tolerance of others found positive results from the Milwaukee Parental Choice Program (MPCP) (Fleming et al. 2014). The authors reported that student voucher status was associated with a 0.15-point increase in the 4-point political tolerance scale and a higher likelihood of stating that their schools promote political tolerance. While this was not an experiment, researchers used a sophisticated algorithm that matched private and public school students on geographic location, baseline test scores and other demographic characteristics. Methodological studies have shown that this type of matching technique is one of the best at replicating experimental results (Bifulco 2012; Cook et al. 2008).

Civic engagement

We identified five studies on the impacts of private school choice on civic engagement. Three studies found positive effects of private school choice (Table 3). Two studies did not find an impact of school choice on engagement. There were two experimental evaluations: one of the New York Choice Scholarships Fund (SCSF) and another of the Children's Scholarship Fund (CSF) of Toledo, Ohio (Bettinger and Slonim 2006; Carlson et al. 2017). The other three programme evaluations examined the MPCP and used quasi-experimental matching methods to determine programme effects on political participation and volunteering (Fleming 2014; Fleming et al. 2014; DeAngelis and Wolf 2016b).

The lab experiment performed by Bettinger and Slonim (2006) found that winning an educational scholarship through the Children's Scholarship Fund in Toledo positively affected a student's charitable activity. Conversely, the authors did not find significant evidence that vouchers affected parents' altruism. Specifically, they found that, in a lab setting, voucher lottery winners gave $4.08 to charity while voucher losers donated only $3.33, a difference of 23 per cent.

Table 3   The effect of school choice on civil engagement

Study	Programme	Type	Design	Finding
Bettinger and Slonim (2006)	CSF Ohio	Charitable giving	RCT	+
Carlson et al. (2017)	SCSF	Voting	RFT	Null
DeAngelis and Wolf (2016b)	MPCP	Voting	Matching QED	Null
Fleming (2014)	MPCP	Political participation	Matching QED	+
Fleming et al. (2014)	MPCP	Political participation, volunteering	Matching QED	+

Note: Null indicates that the study did not detect any statistically significant effect on civic engagement. A box highlighted in grey indicates that the study found statistically significant positive effects on civic engagement.

The random assignment experiment by Carlson et al. (2017) found that the offer of a private school voucher in New York City did not have any impact on voter registration or voter turnout. Moreover, this study did not find any impacts, positive or negative, of the school choice voucher on any of the elections or subgroups examined.

Fleming (2014) used the matched-student data from the evaluation of the MPCP and focused on the resulting political engagement of parents. Fleming found that voucher parents were more than twice as likely to say that they had contacted a government official and had a 7 percentage point higher likelihood of saying that their child's school experience taught them about government. Voucher parents had a 4 percentage point higher likelihood of saying that the government influenced their child's school, indicating that the programme increased the visibility of educational policy to parents. Furthermore, voucher parents had a 9 percentage point higher likelihood of saying that their child's school experience increased their own political activity.

Fleming et al. (2014) used the same MPCP dataset and matching procedure but focused on the political impacts for students. Overall, they found that students in the private school choice programme displayed moderately higher levels of civic skills, political participation and volunteer activity. Their preferred model found that voucher students had an 11 percentage point higher likelihood of stating they would certainly vote in the future and were more likely to take part in civic skill-building activities in school than public school students. Finally, they found that voucher students had an 11 percentage point higher likelihood of volunteering within the previous year and also were more likely to believe in the importance of volunteer activity. When students were asked if they thought they would volunteer as adults, there was no statistically significant effect of private school choice detected.

DeAngelis and Wolf (2016b) used the same student-level dataset from the MPCP evaluation employed in the previous two studies of intentions to vote but found slightly different results regarding actual voting behaviour.

They examined students in 2012 and 2016, when they were around 19–26 years old, and found no difference in voter participation between the students in the school choice programme and the students in public schools. While it is unclear if the MPCP increased voter activity, it is possible that access to the programme developed the citizenship skill of understanding society's expectations regarding civic engagement.

Table 4   The effect of school choice on social order

Study	Programme	Type	Design	Finding
DeAngelis & Wolf (2016a)	MPCP	Adult crime	Matching QED	+

Note: A box highlighted in grey indicates that the study found statistically significant positive effects on social order.

Social order

The least explored area of research within this review is how private school choice relates to social order, perhaps because social order is so difficult to quantify and measure. Criminal activity by young adults is a viable proxy for social order. The only study examining the relationship between private school choice and crime finds that increases in school choice reduce the likelihood of students becoming criminals (DeAngelis and Wolf 2016a). The researchers use the MPCP evaluation dataset and find that participating in the voucher programme for at least four years reduces the likelihood of being accused of any crime by between 21 and 50 percent. Four-year persistence in the programme is also associated with young adults being less than half as likely to be convicted of a misdemeanour or a felony by the time they are around 22–25 years old (Table 4).

Overall results

A majority of the studies find statistically significant positive results, indicating that private school choice leads to improved civic outcomes for individuals and society (Table 5). None of the reviewed studies found statistically significant results indicating that private school choice harmed tolerance of others, charitable giving, political participation, volunteering, civic skills or social order.

Table 5   Summary of results

Outcome	Positive	Null	Negative
Tolerance	3	3	0
Civic engagement	3	2	0
Social order	1	0	0

In particular, half of the six studies examining tolerance found that private school choice increased tolerance, while the remaining half found no significant difference. Three of the five studies examining the effects of private school choice on civic engagement found clearly positive impacts on society through increased political participation, volunteer activity, charitable giving and civic skills. The only study examining impacts on criminal activity found that access to school choice reduced adult crime, leading to improved social order.

Need for further research

While the literature on the impacts of private school choice on student achievement does not suffer from a shortage of studies, the same cannot be said of the research on the social impacts of choice. It is difficult to make an informed policy decision when solely relying on information about student test scores, especially since there are many claims that private schooling can harm society as a whole while benefiting individuals. Surely, if private schooling only benefited individual students by slightly increasing standardised test scores at the expense of widespread intolerance, democratic disengagement and social disorder, policymakers would be well advised to eschew such programmes.

However, if we find sufficient evidence to suggest that private schooling benefits individuals and society overall, we may feel more comfortable with policy proposals leading towards those ends. While this review finds that existing evidence indicates private school choice improves civic outcomes in the US, the evidence is relatively sparse. Additional causal research on all of these topics is especially welcome and highly policy-relevant. Learning more about the impacts of private schooling on society will allow us to understand what type of educational system is necessary for a democratic society to flourish.

Conclusion and policy implications

This review of the literature finds that private school choice programmes in the US are generally beneficial to overall social goals such as tolerance, civic engagement and order. In particular, out of the eleven studies on private school choice that examine these civic outcomes, the impacts are neutral to positive for tolerance, neutral to positive for civic engagement and positive for social order. None of the studies indicates that private school choice has negative effects on civic outcomes. This does not mean that private school choice cannot harm civic outcomes, only that there is no evidence yet that it has done so. Furthermore, the studies included in this review largely focus on the private school choice programmes in Milwaukee and DC, which are not representative of the country as a whole.

The literature on this topic is relatively sparse, and existing evidence only pertains to specific groups of students, so decision-makers should be cautious about using these results for policy decisions. In addition, the effects found in all of these studies are for students that elect to use private school choice programmes. Students left behind in publicly run schools could do worse on civic outcomes through negative peer effects; however, public institutions may also increase their focus on character skills in order to remain competitive. Nonetheless, the current research indicates that private school choice programmes such as vouchers, tuition tax-credits and education savings accounts can improve tolerance of others, civic engagement and social order for children in the US.

Researchers should ask more questions related to the civic outcomes of school choice and education in general. To help researchers do so, decision-makers should focus on policies that improve the amount of information available to researchers on non-academic outcomes of students in the US. In particular, individual student information such as name and date of birth is necessary for researchers to find impacts of school choice programmes on civic outcomes such as political participation and criminal activity. Making such data widely available to researchers will help us further to test the question of whether private school choice advances the public purposes of education.

References

Abdulkadiroglu, A., Pathak, P. A. and Walters, C. R. (2015) School vouchers and student achievement: first-year evidence from the Louisiana Scholarship Program. National Bureau of Economic Research Working Paper 21839.

Apple, M. W. and Beane, J. A. (1995) *Democratic Schools*. Alexandria, VA: Association for Supervision and Curriculum Development.

Artello, K. and Williams, S. (2014) Stress and crime. *The Wiley–Blackwell Encyclopedia of Health, Illness, Behavior, and Society*. Wiley–Blackwell.

Bettinger, E. and Slonim, R. (2006) Using experimental economics to measure the effects of a natural educational experiment on altruism. *Journal of Public Economics* 90(8): 1625–48.

Bifulco, R. (2012) Can non-experimental estimates replicate estimates based on random assignment in evaluations of school choice? A within-study comparison. *Journal of Policy Analysis and Management* 31(3): 729–51.

Berkman, M. and Plutzer, E. (2010) *Evolution, Creationism, and the Battle to Control America's Classrooms*. Cambridge University Press.

Boyles, D. R. (ed.) (2004) *Schools or Markets? Commercialism, Privatization, and School–Business Partnerships*. Mahwah, NJ: Lawrence Erlbaum Associates.

Campbell, D. E. (2002) The civic side of school reform: how do school vouchers affect civic education? Center for the Study of Democratic Politics Working Paper.

Carlson, D., Chingos, M. M. and Campbell, D. E. (2017) The effect of private school vouchers on political participation: experimental evidence from New York City. *Journal of Research on Educational Effectiveness* 10(3): 1–25.

Cheng, H. and DeLany, B. (1999) Quality education and social stratification: the paradox of private schooling in China. *Current Issues in Comparative Education* 1(2): 48–56.

Chubb, J. E. and Moe, T. M. (2011) *Politics, Markets, and America's Schools*. Washington, DC: Brookings Institution Press.

Cook, T. D., Shadish, W. R. and Wong, V. C. (2008) Three conditions under which experiments and observational studies produce comparable causal estimates: new findings from within-study comparisons. *Journal of Policy Analysis and Management* 27(4): 724–50.

Cowen, J. M., Fleming, D. J., Witte, J. F., Wolf, P. J. and Kisida, B. (2013) School vouchers and student attainment: evidence from a state-mandated study of Milwaukee's parental choice program. *Policy Studies Journal* 41(1): 147–68.

DeAngelis, C. A. and Wolf, P. J. (2016a) The school choice voucher: a 'get out of jail' card? EDRE Working Paper 2016-03 (SSRN: https://ssrn.com/abstract=2743541).

DeAngelis, C. A. and Wolf, P. J. (2016b) Can democracy survive private school choice? The effect of the Milwaukee Parental Choice Program on voting behavior. Unpublished Manuscript.

Durkheim, E. (1956) *Education and Sociology.* New York: Simon and Schuster.

Dynarski, M., Rui, N., Webber, A., Gutmann, B. and Bachman, M. (2017) Evaluation of the DC Opportunity Scholarship Program: impacts after one year. NCEE 2017-4022. National Center for Education Evaluation and Regional Assistance.

Filler, L. (ed.) (1983) *Horace Mann on the Crisis in Education.* Rowman & Littlefield.

Finn, C. (2001) Autonomy: an important component for nurses' job satisfaction. *International Journal of Nursing Studies* 38(3): 349–57.

Fleming, D. J. (2014) Learning from schools: school choice, political learning, and policy feedback. *Policy Studies Journal* 42(1): 55–78.

Fleming, D. J., Mitchell, W. and McNally, M. (2014) Can markets make citizens? School vouchers, political tolerance, and civic engagement. *Journal of School Choice* 8(2): 213–36.

Friedman, M. and Friedman, R. (1990) *Free to Choose: A Personal Statement.* Orlando, FL: Houghton Mifflin Harcourt.

Galston, W. (2004) Civic republicanism, political pluralism, and the regulation of private schools. In *Educating Citizens: International Perspectives on Civic Values and School Choice* (ed. P. J. Wolf and S. Macedo). Washington, DC: Brookings Institution Press.

Glenn Jr, C. L. (1987) *The Myth of the Common School.* Amherst, MA: University of Massachusetts Press.

Gutmann, A. (1999) *Democratic Education.* Princeton University Press.

Hirsch Jr, E. D. (2010) *The Schools We Need: And Why We Don't Have Them*. New York: Anchor.

Howell, W. G. and Peterson, P. E. (2006) *The Education Gap: Vouchers and Urban Schools*. Washington, DC: Brookings Institution Press.

Hoxby, C. M. (ed.) (2007) *The Economics of School Choice*. University of Chicago Press.

Ladd, H. F. (2002) School vouchers: a critical view. *Journal of Economic Perspectives* 16(4): 3–24.

Macedo, S. and Wolf, P. J. (2004) School choice, civic values, and problems of policy comparison. In *Educating Citizens: International Perspectives on Civic Values and School Choice* (ed. P. J. Wolf and S. Macedo). Washington, DC: Brookings Institution Press.

Mathews, F. D. (2006) *Reclaiming Public Education by Reclaiming Our Democracy*. Dayton, OH: Kettering Foundation Press.

Mills, J. N. and Wolf, P. J. (2017) The effects of the Louisiana Scholarship Program on student achievement after three years. School Choice Demonstration Project, University of Arkansas, Fayetteville, AR. Education Research Alliance for New Orleans, Tulane University, New Orleans, LA.

Mills, J. N., Cheng, A., Hitt, C., Wolf, P. J. and Greene, J. P. (2016) Measures of student non-cognitive skills and political tolerance after two years of the Louisiana Scholarship Program. Louisiana Scholarship Program Evaluation Report #2. School Choice Demonstration Project, University of Arkansas, Fayetteville, AR. Education Research Alliance for New Orleans, Tulane University, New Orleans, LA.

Molnar, A. (2013) *School Commercialism: From Democratic Ideal to Market Commodity*. New York: Routledge.

Neal, D. (1997) The effects of Catholic secondary schooling on educational achievement. *Journal of Labor Economics* 15(1, Part 1): 98–123.

Neal, D. (2002) How vouchers could change the market for education. *Journal of Economic Perspectives* 16(4): 25–44.

Niskanen, W. A. (1971) *Bureaucracy and Representative Government*. New Brunswick, NJ: Transaction Publishers.

Peterson, P. E. and Campbell, D. E. (2001) An evaluation of the Children's Scholarship Fund. KSG Working Paper RWP02-020.

Rush, B. (1786) Thoughts upon the mode of education proper in a republic. Cited in Sandel (1988: 129).

Saltman, K. J. (2000) *Collateral Damage: Corporatizing Public Schools – A Threat to Democracy*. Lanham, MD: Rowman & Littlefield.

Sandel, M. J. (1988) *Democracy's Discontent: America in Search of a Public Philosophy*. Harvard University Press.

Shakeel, M. D., Anderson, K. P. and Wolf, P. J. (2016) The participant effects of private school vouchers across the globe: a meta-analytic and systematic review. EDRE Working Paper 2016-07 (SSRN: https://ssrn.com/abstract=2777633).

Short, G. (2002) Faith-based schools: a threat to social cohesion? *Journal of Philosophy of Education* 36(4): 559–72.

Smith, A. (1776) *The Wealth of Nations*, Book 1. London: Methuen.

Stewart, T. and Wolf, P. J. (2014) *The School Choice Journey: School Vouchers and the Empowerment of Urban Families*. London: Palgrave Macmillan.

Viteritti, J. P., Walberg, H. J. and Wolf, P. J. (2005) School choice: how an abstract idea became a political reality. *Brookings Papers on Education Policy* (8): 137–73.

Warren, J. R. (2008) *Graduation Rates for Choice and Public School Students in Milwaukee*. Milwaukee: School Choice Wisconsin.

Witte, J. F. (2004) Regulation in public and private schools in the United States. In *Educating Citizens: International Perspectives on Civic Values and School Choice* (ed. P. J. Wolf and S. Macedo). Washington, DC: Brookings Institution Press.

Wolf, P. J., Peterson, P. E. and West, M. R. (2001). Results of a school voucher experiment: the case of Washington, DC after two years. KSG Working Paper RWP02-022.

Wolf, P. J., Kisida, B., Gutmann, B., Puma, M., Eissa, N. and Rizzo, L. (2013) School vouchers and student outcomes: experimental evidence from Washington, DC. *Journal of Policy Analysis and Management* 32(2): 246–70.

Wolfe, A. (ed.) (2009) *School Choice: The Moral Debate*. Princeton University Press.

5 GLOBAL IDEAS, NATIONAL VALUES AND LOCAL POLICIES: ESTONIAN SCHOOL CHOICE POLICY DESIGN

Kaire Põder and Triin Lauri

Introduction

Market elements such as increased consumer choice alongside financial incentives have been advocated in many post-transition East European countries. Estonia is one of the outstanding cases in many respects. However, there is a puzzle. This puzzle relates to Estonia's basic schooling system. Should Estonia proceed down the choice route or will that exacerbate inequality in provision owing to large income disparities and an ever-widening gender gap?

The school choice literature shows that certain policies may bring education systems closer to efficiency with or without having significant impact on equity (Woessmann 2008; Woessmann et al. 2009; Cobb and Glass 2009; Põder et al. 2013; Musset 2012; Lauri and Põder 2013). However, are school choice ideals and policies transferable across cultures? Ball (1998) argues that the historical roots of an educational system, alongside a country's demographics, cultural mix, value system and the extent of social mobility affect the success of new or adopted approaches to schooling initiatives. So is Estonia ready for a school choice revolution?

We present an explorative case study of Estonia's journey around school choice that considers the cross-cultural transferability of school choice policies from neighbouring Europe and the historical dependency of Estonia's schooling system. Policy design and advice is specific to contexts and needs to take into account the historical legacies and family values of a particular country. Is it appropriate, then, for Estonia to borrow policies from countries with difference legacies and values?

Estonia is a country in the Baltic region of northern Europe with borders to the north with the Gulf of Finland and to the west with the Baltic Sea. To the south there is Latvia and to the east Russia. Across the Baltic Sea lie Sweden and Finland. With a population of just over 1.3 million living on the mainland and 2,222 islands, Estonia gained independence from the Soviet Union in 1991. It continued to develop economically through a transparent government and policies that encouraged markets and high levels of economic freedom.

However, as with many post-Soviet transition countries, the positive effects of economic recovery have not been spread equally across all social groups. Estonia's Gini coefficient shows that its inequality level is similar to liberal regimes elsewhere in the European Union. However, when looking at neighbouring Nordic welfare countries such as Sweden and Finland Estonia's Gini index is much higher. Some social groups within Estonia remain at very high risks of living in poverty. Eurostat data show that the distance between the highest and lowest income quintiles is more than six times, which makes Estonia one of a group of eight countries with the highest distance between income quintiles.

This chapter focuses on the cross-cultural transferability of school choice policies and how to design a school choice initiative bearing in mind specific national values and the historical context of schooling. The chapter proceeds as follows. The first section provides an insight into the puzzle. This is that Estonia has shown outstanding – and improving – performances in system level educational indicators, while simultaneously moving towards increasing income disparities. In the second section we describe the historical context and how it continues to inform the underlying principles and characteristics of basic education. Following on from this, the third section considers the choice policies that are emerging in basic education and the influence of European neighbours. The fourth section compares policy recommendations for Estonia's school choice design that appear in the literature, and considers the possible implications. Finally, we discuss and summarise where we are today with school choice in Estonia, and suggest possible ways forward.

Estonia's achievements on the world stage

Estonia is proud of its positioning in international league tables in respect of both educational efficiency (e.g. PISA scores) and equity (e.g. proportion of low achievers). Estonia has shown consistent improvements in its PISA rankings and is ranked in second place in Europe and fourth place overall. As shown in Table 6, Estonia ranked first in Europe in science (third in the world after Singapore and Japan), second in Europe in maths (ninth in the world) and third in reading in Europe (sixth in the world).

Table 6   Top scorers in PISA 2015: average scores for science, reading and maths

Science		Reading		Maths	
Singapore	556	Singapore	535	Singapore	564
Japan	538	Hong Kong	527	Hong Kong	548
Estonia	534	Canada	527	Macau	544
Taiwan	532	Finland	526	Taiwan	542
Finland	531	Ireland	521	Japan	532
Macau	529	Estonia	519	China	531
Canada	528	South Korea	517	South Korea	524
Vietnam	525	Japan	516	Switzerland	521
Hong Kong	523	Norway	513	Estonia	520
China	518	New Zealand	509	Canada	516
Britain	509	Britain	498	Britain	492
US	496	US	497	US	470

Note: Chinese students from Beijing, Shanghai, Jiangsu and Guangzhou took part in the PISA 2015 test.

Source: PISA 2015, OECD.

While international scholars have acknowledged the efficiency, effectiveness and equity of the Estonian education system, paradoxically the quality of teachers and the attractiveness of the teaching profession have been a concern (Eisenschmidt et al. 2015). There are several reasons for this concern. First, teachers are an aging population with an unbalanced gender structure: the average age is close to 50 and the share of women is above 85 per cent (OECD 2017). Second, there is a mismatch between the need for innovative teaching practices and the skills that were acquired by teachers when Estonia was part of the Soviet Union before 1991. Third the teaching profession is not an attractive option for top-quality candidates who can find employment in other professional capacities. Salaries in teaching compare badly with other career options for those with masters qualifications (OECD 2017).

Also, several education 'gaps' have been revealed within the PISA data, including ethnic divisions, regional disparities and the distinction between selective and non-selective schools. So how did we get to where we are? The next section considers the historical legacies underlying the current schooling system in Estonia.

How the current educational system stems from historical legacies

Having a comprehensive schooling system and one that focused on equal opportunities was always part of the Soviet educational rhetoric. The arguments around the struggle between efficiency and equality that shaped the Soviet educational landscape, and hence that of Estonia, are therefore discussed here.

Estonian education is characterised by a comprehensive schooling system with a low share of private schools. The education system is one that is typified by all-through schools, children typically staying in the same school for twelve years. Changes of school are uncommon and they are not encouraged. The system reflects the historical tradition of the agrarian society. Children start school at the age of seven and there are long summer holiday breaks. However, the majority of children under the age of seven and above the age of a year and a half attend kindergarten, following a compulsory curriculum.

Before the nineteenth century most education was carried out in the home. Until the middle of that century three-class village schools were common. Urban education would have been carried out in German or sometimes in Russian/French, and this continued until the twentieth century. It was very difficult for peasants to attend school even though they formed the majority of the population. It is estimated that only 2 per cent of peasant children were enrolled in schooling compared with 70 per cent of the nobility and what are termed the 'non-taxed' citizens (clergy, clerks and the military). Before World War I, when education was not free, it was considered quite elitist, and the main means of social mobility. However, after World War I comprehensive primary education was declared free, and this was quickly followed by the provision of free and compulsory secondary education.

In the USSR, the education system was unified, centralised and state-controlled. In principle, in the period after World War II, the Soviet school system was uniform and all schools offered exactly the same curriculum, approved by the Ministry of Education. In reality, though, school quality differed, and these differences in school quality mainly depended on teacher availability and qualifications. In most cases there were better schools with highly qualified staff in the central areas of metropolitan cities and understaffed schools in rural or industrial areas (Põder et al. 2016). This was not, however, the case in Estonia, where there was a comprehensive schools network in rural areas and teachers were allocated to schools after graduation by the state, and if sent to a rural area would need to teach there. There was therefore little mismatch between rural and urban schooling at this time.

In the 1960s, though, the differentiation of schools was formally recognised, and a new category was introduced – 'specialised schools' – which offered enhanced curricula in modern languages or in the natural sciences (Põder et al. 2016). The enhanced curricula in modern languages emerged because Soviet elites (party elite and professionals) wanted language education for their children. Schools with enhanced curricula in math and physics were all organised by academic elites, their existence justified by considerations of national security and the need for research and development during the Cold War. They were established only in major cities, and their numbers grew gradually. All of these selective schools admitted children based on ability testing or the results of 'Math Olympiads' (ibid.).

However, in the Soviet period Estonian schools were able to keep Estonian as a language of instruction while Russian schools were introduced to serve the educational needs of first-generation immigrants. These immigrants were both military families and relatively low-skilled labour that met the need for the industrialisation that occurred in the 1960s and 70s.

Many industrial towns close to the Russian border became primarily Russian-speaking. However, at the same time the elitist traditions of Estonian schools were being reinforced. Therefore, Estonian urban schools took mostly language profiles and went against the natural science focus of the specialised schools that were found in most Russian urban settings. In the Estonian urban schools selectivity was high, with schools focusing on their historical reputation to attract pupils. These city schools that could use their historical roots typically had served Swedish or German nobility in the past, and most recently the emerging Estonian middle classes.

Schools with Estonian or Russian as their languages of instruction still coexist in today's Estonian education system, regardless of political attempts to integrate the systems. The differences between the performance of children studying in schools offering Estonian-language instruction and those offering Russian-language instruction (hereafter, Estonian and Russian schools) are significant. However, while the ethnic educational gap is closing slightly, the gap between selective and non-selective schools, whether Estonian or Russian, has remained the same, especially in urban areas.

Implicit school choice: policy learning from Europe

School choice is a widespread practice in educational systems, but is also a highly charged ideological battleground. There is broad agreement that school systems need to be improved, but equally broad disagreement about the extent to which choice can produce it. Traditionally in Europe, with some exceptions, where a child lives determines where a child goes to school. Neighbourhood schooling was widely considered the best arrangement for public education. This system was administered either by centrally defined administrative entities as catchment areas or school zones, which determined the school the children in a particular neighbourhood should attend.

Today school choice is widespread, having explicitly (e.g. Sweden or the Netherlands) or implicitly evolved (e.g. Estonia and Russia). While the theoretical literature on choice-based public policy developments emphasises choice-enabled responsiveness to diverse social needs, in the empirical literature efficiency and equity aims of the school choice initiatives dominate. The evidence of choice-related efficiency claims is ambiguous (Teske and Schneider 2001; Woessmann et al. 2009) while the equity problem is widely debated (overview in Musset (2012)). The latter typically hypothesises that choice causes unequal access to education for different families, resulting in educational segregation, i.e. children from 'better' families go to 'better' schools reinforcing the inter-school gap. But this would also be the case for urban and rural disparities as well as schooling by neighbourhood.

However, the meaning, framing and instruments of choice policies vary a lot across countries. In the UK and in other countries where private schooling has had a long tradition, school choice initiatives have generated strong equity concerns (Gorard et al. 2003). In others, policy developments in education have often been triggered by the wave of decentralisation of education as part of a bigger movement in New Public Management (NPM) in the late 1980s and early 1990s. In this context, the problem of school choice often points to the reforms that give parents the right to influence decisions concerning the allocation of pupils to public-sector schools. This development is usually driven by market-based ideology, which assumes that increased competition will generate the incentives that will improve schools and children's achievement (Le Grand 2007; Gingrich 2011). These marketisation initiatives are either exogenous or endogenous (Ball and Youdell 2008), i.e. the marketisation of the public sector in attracting private sector providers to take part in the provision of public services, or the marketisation within the public sector by creating market elements within the public domain.

Although geographical assignment (catchment area or zone-based) is still the main approach in assigning children to schools, there is a major trend in OECD countries to give parents choice beyond their local neighbourhood school. This is done through different schemes such as changing catchment areas, establishing criteria for schools to select their children or making criteria more flexible.

In the case of such school choice policies, the focus is on the admission criteria and enrolment policies of schools, and more specifically, the constraints on parental opportunities to choose to mitigate the potential problem of educational inequality. Cobb and Glass (2009) distinguish between three different forms of school choice: controlled, regulated and unregulated. The former, controlled choice, means that a central authority designs criteria for matching children and schools to oversee the assignment of children to schools with equity in mind and to preserve strong collective guarantee of access (Gingrich 2011). The latter, unregulated choice, has weak if any regulations against cream-skimming and encourages the distribution of the service, based on recipients' risk profile or income (ibid.).

Furthermore, while in some countries school choice has been a clear policy direction intended to improve the quality of education (either in terms of educational efficiency as is the case of NPM-led initiatives or in terms of equity, as is the rhetoric in countries where there is a long tradition of private schooling), in others, similar to the Estonian case, it is rather a 'hidden' consequence of demanding parents and loosened regulations and/or a turn toward more autonomous schools. The empirical findings (Lauri and Põder 2013) reveal that consequent social segregation might be the problem in both 'types' of choice, regardless of where the demand for school choice comes from – from the top (state) or from the bottom (parents). Even countries that have tried to resist choice-supportive policy initiatives have acknowledged that residential choice can segregate by background. Even without any formal choice mechanisms, some parents still find ways to exercise choice, for example, by declaring an address other than their real residence, buying into a neighbourhood to gain access to a particular school, or engaging themselves in the definition of catchment boundaries (Musset 2012).

Although neighborhood schooling is promoted at the state level and education policy initiatives are never framed as enabling choice or enhancing competition, Estonia is one of the 'hidden' choice examples since, in urban areas, parental demand-driven school choice is widely taking place within public schooling. Empirical evidence from 2008 to 2011 (Põder & Lauri 2014a) reveals that in the capital city, Tallinn, more than half of all families have tried to get into popular selective schools (about 10 per cent of all schools). According to the latest PISA, the overall share of selective or partly selective schools in Estonia is between 30 and 70 per cent.[1]

Since the 1990s there have been no distinctively separate reform stages for Estonian education. In general, the system is still comprehensive and neighbourhood schooling is encouraged by regulations. However, education has been a battleground for continuous incremental reforms. From the late 1990s the emergence of an OECD education policy orientation become more apparent. Private schooling has reemerged, but is only partly financed by government[2] and its share is marginal (2–3 per cent of all schools). Government schools have become more autonomous in designing admission policies, in collecting donations and other financial aid from parents, and in decisions on management and content. In urban environments, popular

---

1   Based on the school principals' questionnaire (question SC012Q01TA) in PISA 2015, 26 per cent of schools always admit children based on academic record versus 40 per cent that sometimes and 33 per cent that never admit students based on academic record.

2   The share of public funding of privately operated schools is comparatively high based on OECD data, but schools are allowed to charge tuition fees from families (top-up voucher scheme) making it a common practice among private schools in Estonia.

primary schools may exercise selective intakes by the use of aptitude tests (Põder and Lauri 2014a). Although legal amendments in 2010 have tried to increase the importance of proximity and siblings in school assignment, the current Estonian education system can be characterised as an unregulated choice model in terms of matching students and schools.

Thus, despite the lack of a decisive policy shift toward school choice, the 'inherited' system has gradually become more selective. Starting from 1993, there have simultaneously been inter- and intra-district school practices in place in urban areas. In inter-district schools, parents received the right to apply to a school outside of the catchment area. Thus, the specialist character of some schools has been maintained by reinforcing historically specialised schools by granting them inter-district selective admission. These 'historically elite' schools are located mainly in classical school buildings in city centres. The schools' ability to admit by academic record has resulted in differences in maths performance, especially in towns and cities. The average gap of 11 points of PISA math scores between regular and selective schools is statistically significant.

Selective schools employ decentralised admission without explicit procedures using entrance tests for school entrants (aged 7). Children are pre-trained in prep schools, where children are basically drilled for tests. Põder and Lauri (2014a) show that approximately 70 per cent of the children who have started their schooling in one of the schools in the capital city during 2008–11 participated in at least one of the prep schools.

In general, school choice policy in Estonia can be described as one of implicit or hidden choice, where the official educational agenda favours comprehensive, neighbourhood schooling, but includes publicly funded schools that are highly selective. These schools test children at the start of their school career (6–7 years) and therefore may be considered to be an early tracking or ability grouping system. Cream-skimming is not avoided. The private share of schooling is small and stable. Schools have considerable autonomy in terms of content and admission, and the external accountability mechanisms are visible and emphasised by school league tables.

Controversial policy but good outcomes

Concerns related to the risk of inequality that choice policies arguably entail have motivated authors (Woessmann et al. 2009; Le Grand 2007; Betts and Loveless 2005; Hirsch 2002; Gingrich 2011) to argue that there are various types of 'markets' in welfare policies and it is possible to design an educational market and a school choice policy that fosters equal opportunity without giving up efficiency (outcome orientation).

According to Le Grand (2007) there are at least three important criteria that have to be met for such a policy to work successfully: (1) horizontal diversity (2) minimal 'cream-skimming' and (3) support for parents to make informed choices (parental empowerment). In Estonia, as described in the previous section, there are deficiencies in all three dimensions.

First, there is limited horizontal diversity – schools rely on the same centrally accepted curriculum, most schools are locally governed (limited private ownership), and show little diversity in teaching methods. While the rhetoric of curriculum reforms has been decentralist, it has neither translated into a real shift in power nor increased the professional autonomy of teachers (Erss et al. 2014). Recent reform agendas have tried to minimise the standardisation of the accountability system to emphasise the child-centric approach and profiles. However, the overall system is still quite standardised and the most visible innovations in practices are mainly in the private sphere. Additionally there is a divide between Russian and Estonian schools, the former being more reluctant to implement alternative pedagogical practices and collaborative cultures. In addition to Russian schools' lower mean scores in PISA, their low-performing students belong predominantly to regular (non-selective) schools, while Russian selective schools (those which sometimes or always select) do not perform so badly compared to Estonian schools.[3] However, they have fewer top performers. In general, Estonian selective school students top perform in European comparisons, and are equal to the average Japanese students, while Russian selective school students are comparable to the top performers in the post-Soviet countries (e.g. Slovenia and Poland).

---

3   The mean PISA math scores for regular schools are 480 (Russian schools) and 517 (Estonian schools) compared to selective schools 505 (Russian schools) and 531 (Estonian schools).

It is also worth highlighting that Russian schools have a majority of second-generation immigrants, while first-generation immigrants are relatively equally divided between Estonian and Russian schools. So it can be argued that the lower performance of Russian schools is dependent on the mix of the student body – more immigrants and students of lower socioeconomic status (SES). However, this is not what the diversity literature has brought out. Also selectivity is present in both sides of the language divide. Russian-language schools and students perform worse compared with Estonian peers (the gap is approximately equal to three-quarters of a year of instruction). It can be concluded that in Estonia competition can be described as vertically diversified and not horizontal as recommended by the 'good choice design' scholars.

Second, when looking at selective schools in Estonia that benefit from autonomy, there is a great incentive to compete for the best (higher SES) students. Selective schools are often able to employ motivated teachers and their classes are typically made up of children from homogeneous backgrounds, children from mainly the middle and upper middle strata of society. As a consequence urban selective schools in the capital city (the only city in Estonia which has more than 100,000 inhabitants) perform considerably better than regular schools. These features of uncontrolled choice – segregation of higher SES students and better performance – are features of the Estonian case. Surprisingly, however, this 'cream skimming' policy does not produce considerable effects on total equity and performance indicators, as the PISA results would testify.

Thus, the second criterion recommended for a choice design – opportunities and incentives for selection or cream-skimming should be eliminated – is not met by Estonian school choice policy. But this criterion is not necessarily supported by the public as a whole. It is interesting to note that surveys carried out in selective schools in Tallinn show that parents believe that it is ethically acceptable to use selective admission and that this admission be based on prep schooling. This vital beginning then paves the way, it is believed, to success by climbing the social mobility ladder (Haugas 2016).

Third, the criterion of support for parents to make informed choice (parental empowerment) is weak in Estonia. Põder and Lauri (2014a) show that dwelling in the centre of the city increases the probability of being accepted into a selective school owing to the availability of prep schooling in the capital. Living in the capital is a proxy for family wealth and it should be noted that the educational attainment of parents is also an indicator positively associated with access to selective schooling. Where does that leave choice for the remainder of parents who cannot live in the city, and do not themselves have high educational attainment levels that could increase the likelihood of their children being able to attend a school of their choice? There is no counselling for parents either by the municipalities or by schools around how to make 'informed' choices. Indeed, parents typically choose schools by consulting league tables that indicate state exam results or by following social media. The linguistic divide in Estonia also hinders rather than fosters choice.

The years 2008–10 can be described as the 'pre-market residential choice' period. During this period in Tallinn, the background characteristics of parents were of statistical significance on school attended. After 2010, after the regulations around choice were lifted, background characteristics became less important, but the mother's education attainment level became more significant regarding choice (Põder and Lauri 2014b). Looking at family profiles shows that the chance of being accepted into a selective school is relatively low if the mother's educational attainment does not meet certain criteria.

To summarise, it would seem that the unregulated school choice policy that operates within Estonia today and is rooted in the historical context of the education system does not abide by the three rules recommended by Le Grand (2007) for a school choice policy that fosters equal opportunity without jeopardising efficiency. To remind the reader, the three important criteria that have to be met for such a policy to work successfully are (1) horizontal diversity, (2) minimal 'cream- skimming' and (3) support for parents to make informed choice (parental empowerment).

So, as mentioned earlier, there is a puzzle. While deviating from the recommended choice design, Estonia is doing well in terms of most of the measurable educational outcomes – educational efficiency, equity and effectivity. There are some concerns related to regional, ethnic and selective vs. non-selective education gaps, but the overall outcome regarding student achievements is one of the best in Europe. However, whether this success is fostered by the current choice design or whether the choice design is undermining the potential success of a schooling system which could be attaining better results, is open to question and therefore further and more detailed research.

Conclusion

In our exploratory analysis we have examined the twofold puzzle of Estonia: how increasing income disparities are not producing educational inequality, and how controversial choice policy can still be relatively good at producing efficient and equitable educational results.

We rested our discussion on the empirical insights of the Estonian case on the theoretical platform that choice is not necessarily harmful for educational equity. However, we made the argument that the equity-enhancing capacity of school choice policy is dependent on the specific configurations – policy design and its interaction with case specificity, namely historical legacies and institutions, values and beliefs about the transformation mechanism that generate social mobility. The literature demonstrates that if we only take into account the effect of policy instruments (and not case specificities) there are several school choice policy designs that do well in terms of both educational efficiency and equity. The most consistent are school choice policies that combine the operation of private providers with public funding, or school autonomy in combination with an accountability system in diversifying the school system and enhancing parental opportunities to choose a school for their child.

In addition to these criteria, to mitigate the problems of unequal educational opportunities, it is necessary for school choice policy to limit the school's opportunities for early selection and ability-grouping.

While insights from the literature indicate that ungoverned school choice intensifies segregation problems and these tend to be more severe in ungoverned and hidden-choice environments as compared to overt choice, we emphasise the importance of alternatives (i.e. real choice) in explaining the equity-enhancing abilities of school choice. In the Estonian case we see no explicit policy design. Instead, early ability grouping by schools, creating divides between selective and regular schools or Russian and Estonian schools, is implemented. However, a family's drive and motivation to contribute to the overall social mobility of their children either by pushing them to achieve and compete, which has reinforced the historical split between elite and non-elite schools, is producing results. At least this is what we see in PISA scores. Whether this turns into long-run success or contributes to the future human capital or happiness of the child is a question that needs further study.

Thus, the configurational approach supports the proposition that educational outcomes can be case-specific and that policy instruments such as diversity of the school system, early tracking and ability grouping and parental empowerment work in combination. Above all we argue that these policy instruments produce outcomes of educational equity and efficiency in interaction with case-specific historical and institutional contexts. Our Estonian case study reveals that outlier status in a country-comparative framework cannot be explained by standard policy recommendations. Instead, there are underlying patterns of historical and social institutions that drive results in combination with (or despite) a strange mix of policy instruments.

In conclusion, we see that the 'how to choose' question remains a challenge in designing good educational policy, while 'whether to choose' has lost its significance. The latter means that choice has been imputed to the education governance systems either explicitly or implicitly. Thus we see the question of 'how to choose' instead of 'whether to choose' is of the utmost importance in contemporary public policy. Investigating the complex constellations of design and context is a promising research avenue in order to search for equity-enhancing choice designs.

References

Ball, S. (1998) Big policies/small world: an introduction to international perspectives in education policy. *Comparative Education* 34(20): 119–30.

Ball, S. J. and Youdell, D. (2008) *Hidden Privatisation in Education.* Brussels: Education International.

Betts, J. and Loveless, T. (eds) (2005) *Getting Choice Right: Ensuring Equity and Efficiency in Education Policy.* Washington, DC: Brookings Institution Press.

Cobb, C. D. and Glass, G. V. (2009) School choice in a post-desegregation world. *Peabody Journal of Education* 84: 262–78.

Eisenschmidt, E., Ruus, V.-R. and Poom-Valickis, K. (2015) Õpe-
    tajahariduse perspektiivid – olukord ja väljakutsed (The per-
    spectives and state of the art of teacher education in Estonia).
    Riigikogu Toimetised 31: 51–69 (in Estonian).
Erss, M., Mikser, R., Löfström, E., Ugaste, A., Rõuk, V. and Jaani, J.
    (2014) Teachers' views of curriculum policy: the case of Esto-
    nia. *British Journal of Educational Studies* 62(4): 393–411.
Gingrich, J. R. (2011) *Making Markets in the Welfare State: The Pol-
    itics of Varying Market Reforms.* Cambridge University Press.
Gorard, S., Taylor, C. and Fitz, J. (2003) *School Markets and Choice
    Policies.* Routledge Falmer: London and New York.
Haugas, S. (2016) *Lapsevanemate koolivalikuprotsess ja peam-
    ised determindadid – Tallinna selehtiivsete koolide näide* (The
    process and the main determinants of parents' school choice
    – an example of Tallinn's selective schools). Bachelor thesis,
    Tallinn University (in Estonian).
Hirsch, D. (2002) *What Works in Innovation in Education. School:
    A Choice of Directions.* Centre for Educational Research and
    Innovation. Paris: OECD.
Lauri, T. and Põder, K. (2013) School choice policy – seeking to
    balance educational efficiency and equity. A comparative
    analysis of 20 European countries. *European Educational Re-
    search Journal* 12: 534–52.
Le Grand, J. (2007) *The Other Invisible Hand: Delivering Public
    Services through Choice and Competition.* Princeton Univer-
    sity Press.
Musset, P. (2012) *School Choice and Equity: Current Policies in
    OECD Countries and a Literature Review.* OECD Education
    Working Papers 66.

OECD (2017) Mathematics performance (PISA) (indicator) (https://doi.org/10.1787/04711c74-en).

Põder, K. and Lauri, T. (2014a) When public acts like private: the failure of Estonia's school choice mechanism. *European Educational Research Journal* 13: 220–34.

Põder, K. and Lauri, T. (2014b) Will choice hurt? Compared to what? A school choice experiment in Estonia. *Journal of School Choice: International Research and Reform* 8(3): 446–74.

Põder, K., Kerem, K. and Lauri, T. (2013) Efficiency and equity within European education systems and school choice policy: bridging qualitative and quantitative approaches. *Journal of School Choice: Research, Theory, and Reform* 7(1): 1–36.

Põder, K., Lauri, T., Ivaniushina, V. and Alexandrov, D. (2016) Family background and school choice in cities of Russia and Estonia: selective agenda of the Soviet past and present. *Studies of Transition States and Societies* 8(3): 5–28.

Teske, P. and Schneider, M. (2001) What research can tell policymakers about school choice. *Journal of Policy Analysis and Management* 20(4): 609–31.

Woessmann, L. (2008) How equal are educational opportunities? Family background and student achievement in Europe and the United States. *Zeitschrift für Betriebswirtschaft* 78(1): 45–70.

Woessmann, L., Lüdemann, E., Schütz, G. and West, M. R. (2009) *School Accountability, Autonomy, and Choice around the World* Cheltenham: Edward Elgar.

6 SCHOOL CHOICE IN LIBERIA

Pauline Dixon and Steve Humble

Introduction

It is often assumed that governments should provide, regulate and finance education. There are several economic arguments put forward to support this premise: that education is a public good, a merit good, has beneficial externalities to a population and children need protecting from irresponsible parents. But even if all of these economic arguments hold true – and there is contention around this – what happens when governments cannot afford to provide schooling for children within their own countries? What happens when a country is plagued by badly functioning public institutions include the judiciary? What happens when a country has recently emerged from civil war? What happens when governments fail to provide quality education for all?

School choice programmes operate around the world, providing choice to parents either by default or design. This chapter sets out empirical evidence from Liberia, a post-conflict country, setting out an example of school choice that has evolved both by default and more recently by design.

There are three parts to this essay. The first considers how historical and cultural contexts influence schooling provision in a country such as Liberia. The second sets out two aims: the first, to explore the provision of schooling in Monrovia, the capital of Liberia; the second to investigate how parents choose from an array of schools, given their family background and their child's characteristics. The third part describes the current public–private partnership initiative being trialled by the Liberian government, Partnership Schools for Liberia (PSL), that is outsourcing government schools to private contractors. The chapter then concludes by setting out how evidence-based policy initiatives could support parents to be active choosers.

Historical contexts

In 1822, the American Colonization Society (ACS) founded Liberia as a colony for freed former slaves being repatriated to Africa from the US. Both freeborn African-Americans and freed slaves settled among the sixteen indigenous population groups that already inhabited Liberia and become known as the Americo-Liberians (UNESCO 2011a). In 1847 the colony became an independent nation. With the Americo-Liberians taking control, they set up, in Monrovia, services and infrastructure that benefited their own self-interest and domination. The rural population failed to benefit from this building of political, economic and social institutions, which resulted in marginalisation and tension built fragility among the population. Schools were set up to cater for the children of Americo-Liberians; indigenous children were not allowed to attend these schools and therefore gained education outside this formal system (Moran 2006).

This domination by the minority elite lasted until 1979 when Samuel Doe staged a military coup and assassinated the incumbent president. However, domination just changed hands to the Krahn tribe, which represented only 4 per cent of the population. After around ten years, civil war broke out and took place between 1989 and 1996 and between 1999 and 2003. Conflict in Liberia has stemmed from high levels of poverty, inequality and unequal access to assets and opportunities, including access to education.

Civil wars cause devastation and in Liberia this included the collapse of the economy, destruction of physical infrastructure, institutions and basic services, including schooling. It has been estimated that a third of government schools and a quarter of community schools were destroyed during the civil war. Schools were looted and demolished with teachers fleeing and children abducted to be conscripted into the fighting forces (UNESCO 2011b). As a consequence according to the Government of Liberia (2008: 185) 'the majority of Liberia's young people have spent more time engaged in war than in school'. One third of Liberia's population have had no education, 31 per cent have only experienced primary schooling with 36 per cent having had secondary and in some cases tertiary education.

School choice for the poor in the slums of Monrovia

Provision of schooling in Monrovia

After several failed government education recovery initiatives and schooling becoming compulsory and free at the primary level, different school management types took up the initiative to supply schooling in order to meet the demand. This part of the essay considers the schooling landscape of seven designated slums of Monrovia. Monrovia has the greatest population density in the country of around 1,500 people per square mile with one third of the population of Liberia residing in the capital (LIGIS 2009).

Table 7   Characteristics of child's household by type of school attended

Item	Govt	PP	FBM	Com.	Total
Language spoken at home (% of respondents)					
English	78.7	77.3	76.6	75.7	77.0
Grebo	8.5	8.7	8.3	3.9	8.1
Kru	3.0	1.0	2.0	4.9	2.2
Kpelle	1.8	3.1	2.6	2.9	2.7
Other	8.0	9.9	10.5	12.6	10.0
Total number in household (mean)	5.85	5.32	5.31	5.46	5.40
Children in household (mean)	3.67	3.03	3.10	3.34	3.18
Highest household education level (%)					
No schooling or primary only	62.5	58.9	61.1	56.7	60.4
Above primary	37.5	41.1	38.9	43.3	39.6

Occupation (%)					
Employed (labourers, fishermen, market)	73.1	79.1	77.7	76.0	77.3
Unemployed	26.9	20.9	22.3	24.0	22.7
Mean monthly household income (LRD; £)	5,175 (£44.61)	6,930 (£59.74)	7,462 (£64.33)	6,571 (£56.65)	6,943 (£59.85)
Mean monthly household expenditure (LRD; £)	3,471 (£29.92)	5,754 (£49.60)	4,626 (£39.88)	5,701 (£49.15)	4,829 (£41.63)
Mean monthly school cost (LRD; £)	198 (£1.71)	615 (£5.30)	573 (£4.94)	553 (£4.77)	531 (£4.58)
Household assets (%)					
Generator	8.3	20.9	26.8	17.3	22.0
TV	9.4	23.3	29.7	19.2	24.5
Cellphone	70.6	76.7	77.8	76.0	76.4
Computer	2.4	4.7	4.2	8.7	4.5
Motorbike	0.6	2.7	4.2	2.9	3.2
Car	1.2	2.4	2.7	1.9	2.4

Notes: Currency: 116 (Liberian dollars) = £1; monthly expenditure is based on cost for food, fuel, rent and mobile phone charges; Govt, government; PP, private provider; FBM, faith-based mission; Com., community; .

After carrying out a systematic sweep of seven designated slums[1] in Monrovia, a total of 432 schools were located (Tooley and Longfield 2014, 2017). Out of this total the government ran only two. The management types serving these communities included private proprietor, non-governmental organisations (NGOs), mission schools representing religious beliefs in Liberia (Methodist, Catholic, Baptist, Lutheran, Islamic, Seventh Day Adventist, Assembly of God

---

1   Doe Community, Clare Town, Westpoint, New Kru Town, Logan Town, Chicken Soup Factory and St Paul Bridge Community. The 2008 National Housing and Population Census show these to be among the poorest communities of Monrovia (http://microdata.worldbank.org/index.php/catalog/2098/study-description).

and Inland Mission) and community schools. The largest provider was found to be the private proprietor, accounting for around 57 per cent of the schools catering for 61 per cent of the pupils. The supply of schools therefore has risen owing to the inability of the Liberian government to provide or fund schooling. Irrespective of this, parents still want their children to be educated. The lack of educational opportunities would only exacerbate fractious tensions and the possibility of returning to civil war, an undesirable consequence of an uneducated populace.

Parental preferences, household background and child characteristics

Carrying out household interviews with parents concerning schooling decisions and choices allows evidence to be gathered about revealed preferences. The data reported here covered children from 1,236 households in which interviews were carried out with parents of children attending schools in the seven slums in Monrovia. The survey focused on the decisions parents made for their eldest 'in school' child. The average age of these children was around 10.4 years and just over half were girls (Humble and Dixon 2017). Looking at the household characteristics of the families by the type of school attended shows great similarity (Table 7). These include the language spoken at home, the majority (77 per cent) speaking English, and the number of children and adults in the household (averaging 3.18 children and 5.4 adults). The great majority (77.3 per cent) of fathers reported working as unskilled labourers, market traders and fishermen with most families (63.7 per cent) having one earning family member. All households that participated in this survey stated that they had an income, which allowed all schools to be an option for their eldest child. As for possessions, 76.4 per cent of the families owned a mobile phone though only 4.5 per cent had a computer and 4 per cent a motorbike.

As well as finding out about family background and wealth, parents were asked to provide the three main reasons for choosing the school for their eldest child. Providing definitions for these preferences can be quite subjective. Parents use informal methods to quantify preference. The six most-cited preferences and the interpretation provided by parents were:

- *Affordability.*
- *Strong disciplinary environment* – fostered around reputation and trust.
- *Safe and close to home* – this often implies that the school is within walking distance and trusted by the community.
- *School reputation* – emphasis is put upon parents knowing the school leaders and their standing within and commitment to the community.
- *Academic performance* – based around examination results as well as homework frequency and teacher feedback and marking of work;
- *Quality of teaching* – typically implies that teachers attend school regularly and are committed and caring to their pupils.

Table 8 . **Estimates of the empirical model**

	PP	FBM	Community
Parental preferences			
Affordability	0.232*** (0.356)	0.192***(0.324)	0.439**(0.432)
Strong disciplinary environment	0.563*(0.349)	0.571*(0.325)	0.818(0.430)
Safe and close to home	1.812(0.371)	2.045**(0.340)	4.450***(0.469)
School reputation	0.520 (0.365)	0.549*(0.335)	0.807(0.447)
Academic performance	0.979(0.388)	0.821(0.359)	1.113(0.476)
Quality of teaching	1.363(0.371)	1.556(0.341)	1.692(0.447)
Household characteristics			
Gender (Girl = 1)	1.140(0.235)	0.791(0.214)	1.627*(0.284)
Age	0.247***(0.051)	0.379***(0.048)	0.403***(0.058)
Number of children in family	0.448***(0.145)	0.523***(0.134)	0.709(0.176)
Total number in family	2.214**(0.110)	1.750**(0.103)	1.343(0.136)
School costs	2.702***(0.088)	2.029***(0.080)	1.886***(0.104)
Wealth 1	1.374**(0.015)	1.740***(0.014)	1.324*(0.018)
Wealth 2	0.986(0.017)	1.153(0.015)	1.465(0.016)
Family expenditure	1.402(0.310)	1.350(0.285)	1.201(0.366)
Family income	1.347(0.261)	1.697**(0.239)	1.489(0.309)
Highest household education	1.018(0.239)	1.020(0.218)	0.892(0.287)
Occupation	1.311(0.286)	0.983(0.268)	1.176(0.342)
Proportion of non-gov/gov	1.372***(0.012)	1.557***(0.011)	1.421***(0.018)
Constant	1.507(1.700)	0.268(1.572)	0.654(1.947)

Analysis includes 1,236 observations. Omitted category for school type: in government school. Standard errors in parentheses. *p < 0.10; **p < 0.05; ***p < 0.01. Wealth 1 indicates families who have a greater share of luxury and consumer goods, Wealth 2 are families whose possessions are more closely linked with daily paid labour.

The three most important preferences stated by the majority of parents were 'quality of teaching' (79.9 per cent), 'safe and close to home' (63.9 per cent) and 'strong disciplinary environment' (53.3 per cent).

Assuming that all parents had the option to select any of the school types, an estimation of the multinomial logistic regression model allows testing for household preferences and demographics that affect the choice of attending different school management types.

The coefficient estimates of the discrete choice model in terms of odds ratios (with the base group being government schools) are shown in Table 8. Where the odds ratio is less than 1, parents are expressing a preference for government over the named school type. Asterisks signify statistically significant preferences and household characteristics. There are four parental preferences around school choice that are statistically significant. Parents who state that affordability is a preference are more likely to send their child to a government school than all other types of school. Regarding strong disciplinary environment and school reputation, parents are more likely to send their child to government rather than private or faith-based mission when stating their preferences. Parents who stated a preference when selecting schools by them being 'safe and close to home' are more likely to send their child to a faith-based mission or community school. Individual characteristics show a general pattern across all non-government schools. There is an increase in the likelihood of parents sending a child to a government school as the child gets older and there are more children in the family. The increased economic wellbeing of a family tends to increase the likelihood of a parent choosing a non-government school. Parents who send their children to private proprietor, faith-based mission and community schools prefer to keep their child in non-government education as the number of government schools increases in their community. This research is unique in that it considers the choice process undertaken by poor parents to inform schooling decisions. This body of information as a whole implies that parents living in difficult circumstances, having faced the troubles associated with war and conflict, are making informed choices using a variety of information.

Partnership schools for Liberia

It has been acknowledged that education plays a central role regarding a country's stability and development (Ndaruhut-se et al. 2011; Pavanello and Othieno 2008). Indeed, some attribute civil wars in countries such as Liberia not only to decades of poor governance but also the lack of access to education for the young (Humphreys and Weinstein 2004). Neglect of education can create large cohorts of unemployed, illiterate young people who then are more likely to become conscripts into criminal, corrupt and anti-democratic organisations. In September 2016 the Liberian Education Minister, George K. Werner, under the leadership of the Liberian President Ellen Johnson Sirleaf and with the help of ARK (Absolute Return for Kids, a British education group) delegated the management of 93 government primary and pre-primary schools to eight private bodies.[2] These

---

2   Bridge International Academies (23 schools), BRAC (20 schools), Omega Schools (19 schools), Street Child (12 schools), More than Me (6 schools), Rising Academies (5 schools), Youth Movement for Collective Action (4 schools) and Stella Maris (4 schools).

'contractors' include for-profit and not-for-profit companies and charities, the majority already established in either the school sector or working with marginalised people living in poor circumstances. These contractors are responsible for the daily management of their schools and are provided funding on a per-pupil basis from the Liberian Government.

Academics from the University of California and the Center for Global Development are undertaking a three-year randomised evaluation of the Partnership Schools for Liberia (PSL) pilot. The first-year results have now been published (Romero et al. 2017). The findings show that on average, partnership schools improve teaching and learning. There has been an increase in the quality of teacher instruction. Teachers are more likely to be at their posts in school and engaged in instruction than in non-PSL schools. Children in partnership schools spend twice as much time learning each week, resulting in their making roughly seven months more progress in English and maths compared with children learning in ordinary government schools.

Liberia's government spends $50 (USD) per pupil per year in ordinary government schools. The PSL schools receive an extra $50 per pupil on top of this. Some of the private contractors have used their own funds as well as philanthropic contributions to top up the amount spent per pupil with a range from $57 by Youth Movement for Collective Action to Bridge International Academies spending $663 per pupil.

Management techiques have included the removal of some government schoolteachers in PSL schools and bringing in new ones (Bridge International Academies removed

50 per cent of their government teachers). Terminating a teacher's contract is very difficult in such situations. Therefore the removal of teachers from PSL schools could imply these teachers gaining employment in other public schools or actually being paid for not teaching in a school at all.[3] This could therefore be seen as a redistribution of poorly performing teachers to other government schools, causing negative side effects in the system as a whole.

Both parents and children who attend PSL schools have indicated increased happiness and satisfaction with the education being received now they are being schooled in privately managed government schools. It will be interesting to see how this publicly funded, privately provided education scheme unfolds over the next few years and how these private contractors expand choice, allowing for social benefit and schools that tailor to their local environments.

Summary

In this chapter evidence has been considered in order to explore how schooling is expanding in the context of Liberia, a post-conflict country, and one of the poorest in the world. The causes of conflict often stem from high levels of poverty, inequality and unequal access to assets and opportunities. Research shows that poor parents, having suffered the torments of war, are active choosers when it comes to schooling for their children. Parental preferences

---

3   https://www.brookings.edu/blog/future-development/2017/10/05/
    new-research-on-public-private-partnerships-in-education-in-libe-
    ria-and-pakistan/

are typically informed by the environment and context. Focus is often on trust, reputation, caring and commitment in the community itself. Within the slums of Monrovia schooling is booming with a plethora of different school management types offering a range of provision from which to choose. It is not only the market that is responding to the demand for schooling. The Liberian government is also well aware of the importance of schooling to foster success and stability. It has therefore implemented Partnership Schools for Liberia (PSL), Africa's first fee-free national public–private partnership for basic education. The aim is to improve both enrolment and learning outcomes that currently the government system cannot deliver. In time, if PSL proves to be successful, scalable and sustainable, this can only increase choice for parents. With both the market and PSL working hand in hand, this will allow for a range of schools competing in order to raise the bar and standards of education throughout the system.

References

Government of Liberia (2008) *Poverty Reduction Strategy (PRS)*. Monrovia: Government of Liberia.

Humble, S. and Dixon, P. (2017) School choice, gender and household characteristics: evidence from a household survey in a poor area of Monrovia, Liberia. *International Journal of Educational Research* 84: 13–23.

Humphreys, M. and Weinstein, J. (2004) What the fighters say: a survey of ex-combatants in Sierra Leone. CGSD Working Paper 20, Colombia University, New York.

Liberia Institute of Statistics and Geo-Information Services (LISGIS) (2009) *2008 Population and Housing Census: Final Results*. Monrovia: LIAGIS.

Moran, M. (2006) *Liberia: The Violence of Democracy*. Philadelphia, PA: University of Pennsylvania Press.

Ndaruhutse, S., Mansoor, A., Chandran, R., Cleaver, F., Dolan, J., Sondorp, E. and Vaux, T. (2011) State-building, peace-building and service delivery in fragile and conflict-affected states: literature review (Final report). Reading, UK: CfBT Education Trust.

Pavanello, S. and Othieno, T. (2008) Improving the provision of basic services for the poor in fragile environments: education sector international literature review. Report prepared for the AusAID Office of Development Effectiveness. London: ODI.

Romero, M., Sandefur, J. and Aaron, W. (2017) Can outsourcing improve Liberia's schools? Preliminary results from year one of a three year randomised evaluation of Partnership Schools for Liberia. Working Paper 462, Center for Global Development.

Tooley, J. and Longfield, D. (2017) *Education, War and Peace: The Surprising Success of Private Schools in War-Torn Countries*. London: Institute of Economic Affairs.

Tooley, J. and Longfield, D. (2014) Private education in low-income areas of Monrovia: school and household surveys. Working Paper, E. G. West Centre, Newcastle.

UNESCO (2011a) *Education and Fragility in Liberia*. Paris: UNESCO.

UNESCO (2011b) *The Hidden Crisis: Armed Conflict and Education, EFA Global Monitoring Report*. Paris: UNESCO.

7 POOR PARENTS ARE CAREFUL CHOOSERS: DISPELLING THE MYTH THAT SCHOOL CHOICE HARMS THE POOR

M. Danish Shakeel and Patrick J. Wolf

Introduction

Lower educational achievement, attainment and quality of schooling are often associated with poverty. The lack of access to financial resources often acts against the academic aspirations of a poor[1] family. As a solution, governments and international aid agencies tend to call for more public education as the best solution to help poor families (Dixon 2013). Government schools enjoy financial, legal and infrastructural support from the state. These schools also benefit from government's ability to address information asymmetries through centralised data management. Thus most international aid agencies focus their attention on the public system of education.

From the perspective of better-resourced public schools, it may seem unlikely that poor families would adequately

---

1 Here and throughout this chapter we use the term 'poor' exclusively to mean low-income. Thus, a 'poor student' should be understood to be a student with a limited income, not a student who is ineffective (i.e. 'poor') at school.

benefit from less-resourced private schools of choice, especially in developing countries. Nor does it seem possible that poor parents would be good at making quality school choices, because of a lack of quality information or their assumed inability to disentangle complex information about school quality. If these arguments were true, rigorous experimental evidence and field work would provide evidence against school choice for poor families.

Public schools draw most of their funding from the state through taxation. Private schools draw most of their revenue through tuition fees paid by parents. School funding in both the public and private sectors may also come through secular or religious philanthropic sources. Although it seems that public schools have crucial advantages that should lead them to be higher in quality than private schools, the evidence seems to refute that hypothesis. In developing countries, publicly funded schools tend to be low quality because of teacher absenteeism, bureaucratic corruption and a lack of accountability to parents (Dixon 2013; Tooley 2009; Chaudhury et al. 2006). The gap between public and private school quality is smaller in developed countries than in developing countries because developed countries have more resources, better educational infrastructure, and less corruption in public education systems. Yet, even government schools in developed countries are marred by problems of bureaucracy and the influence of special interest groups (such as teachers' unions) that hinder reform (Chubb and Moe 2011). The public school system often acts as a monopoly. School-level behavioural and learning problems continue to exist because of school selection based on residential assignment, lack of easy exit options, unavailability of quality alternatives and a lack of accountability to families.

We dispel the myth that poor families are incapable of choosing schools effectively and hence their choices harm their children. In the sections that follow, we discuss how poor parents select schools and provide evidence on educational outcomes from those selections. We also briefly mention the growth of educational market share for schools of choice serving poor families around the world. We establish that, far from being a problem, school choice acts to empower poor families.

Private school choice programmes for poor families

Low-income families around the world are experiencing greater access to private school choice. The availability of school choice programmes is increasing in the US, with participation by poor parents in such programmes especially strong (EdChoice 2017). School choice has existed to a greater extent in Europe than in North America through both government and philanthropic efforts (Glenn and Candal 2012; Wolf and Macedo 2004). The European schooling system has also seen an increase in Islamic schooling with the increase in Muslim immigration (Dronkers 2016). There has also been an increase in availability of schooling for non-Semitic religions in Europe (Berner 2017). In some cases, the European nations allow faith-based instruction within the public school system.

Although forms of choice such as Charter Schools exist within the traditional public school system in the US, it is clear that most European nations have done far more to help families to educate their children in line with their beliefs and traditions.

Some Latin American governments have policies that promote private school choice for poor families. Chile has had a universal school voucher programme since 1981 (Mizala and Romaguera 2000). Colombia operates a private school choice programme limited to poor families (Angrist et al. 2002). In developing countries poor parents have taken their children's education in their own hands by sending them, at their own expense, to low-cost private schools which are often not under the legal framework of the state (Dixon 2013; Tooley 2012). The proportion of private school enrolment in developing countries is two to three times the private enrolment share in developed countries (Angrist et al. 2002). This fact alone dispels the myth that poor parents do not have private school choice. Not only do poor parents have choice, they create choice out of their own limited resources when the state's free school system is unable to deliver quality.

How poor parents select schools

According to Fuller and Elmore (1996: 3), 'choice schemes assume that the family is highly rational, acts from clear preferences, and is able to effectively demand action from local schools and teachers.' Critics of school choice argue that poor parents are not rational and well-informed choosers and hence their choices will not be linked to academic quality.

Poor parents select schools of choice for a variety of reasons. Academic quality, religion, safety and cultural values are often common reasons for school selection by poor parents (Schneider et al. 1998; Peterson and Campbell 2001; Teske and Schneider 2001; Witte 2000; Martinez et al. 1995; Humble and Dixon 2017; Dixon and Humble 2017). Poorly resourced parents say that they value academic quality as much as better-resourced parents (Farkas and Johnson 1998; Martinez et al. 1995). Hamilton and Guin (2005: 43) state:

> Studies of intra- and inter-district choice, as well as of charter schools and vouchers, all report parents citing measures of academic quality as a primary reason for choosing their child's school.

Lovenheim and Walsh (2017) report that expansions in school choice programmes are positively associated with the frequency with which parents collect data about local school quality, suggesting that the availability of choice options incentivises parents to engage in a school search process.

Academic quality is difficult to measure or understand completely. Poor parents tend to estimate it through proxy variables such as the academic achievements of a school's peer group, class sizes, academic standards and curriculum (Abdulkadiroglu et al. 2017; Hamilton and Guin 2005; Dixon et al. 2017). Although economically disadvantaged families identify a lack of money as the key challenge to access quality education, both parents and students from these families report that they value strong relationships with school faculty and administration (Stewart et al. 2010). Thus, schools of choice are likely to be accountable to poor parents as a result of the students' and families' regular interactions with school personnel.

Switching schools disrupts student learning (Cowen et al. 2012; Elacqua et al. 2004; Hanushek et al. 2004). Any school switch requires that the student adjust to their new school. The launch or expansion of school choice programmes further requires that schools adjust to a new set of students. An initial decline in student learning seems inevitable under such situations (Mills and Wolf 2017a). A better way to address such a concern is to look at the impact on student learning over time, as parental behaviour is likely to develop with the experience of their child's schooling (Mills and Wolf 2017b). A meta-analysis of school voucher test score impacts shows that learning growth tends to adjust with time after an initial dip following the school switch (Shakeel et al. 2016).

Poor families also value non-academic aspects of schools, especially safety (Stewart and Wolf 2016; Howell and Peterson 2006). The National Center for Education Statistics (NCES) report on *Indicators of School Crime and Safety: 2015* shows that public schools in the US have higher rates of crime and lower rates of safety than private schools (Zhang et al. 2016). It is not rational to evaluate a parental choice merely on the basis of test scores and ignoring safety concerns. Poor parents expressed satisfaction with school safety even when the initial year of a school choice intervention yielded negative impacts on maths test scores (Dynarski et al. 2017). Using nationally representative surveys for private and public school principals in the US, Shakeel and DeAngelis (2017) find that principals in private schools are more likely to report less strict disciplinary controls, suggesting that such arrangements are less necessary in private schools. They conclude that private schools may offer a better school environment and safety than public schools.

Access to better information about schools and the level of parental education affect the decision of a family to participate in a school choice programme (Hamilton and Guin 2005). The lack of access to quality information and lower levels of parental education may pose a problem when little information is exchanged between parents and school personnel. Using data from the second-year experimental evaluation of the Washington Scholarship Fund, a privately funded partial-tuition voucher programme, Kisida and Wolf (2010) find that the availability of choice increased matching between parents' responses and school-reported data about school size and class size. This tends to support the view that school choice is not simply about selection of schools but is a journey of learning about schools that empowers poor families (Stewart and Wolf 2016).

School choice provides incentives for increased parental involvement, which may reduce inequities created as a result of stratification by level of parental education. Even if only a small proportion of parents in a school of choice are actively involved in information exchange with the school authorities, the larger group of not very actively involved parents may reap the benefit (Schneider et al. 1998). In responding to the demands of the active parents that Schneider et al. call 'marginal choosers', school personnel benefit the children of not very active parents. Just as not every person who buys an automobile is an auto mechanic, the fact that some car buyers are auto mechanics means that cars need to be built to the exacting standards of such 'marginal choosers', to the benefit of all. Such an opportunity does not exist for the not very actively involved parents in the public school system because parents cannot exit the school system when faced by poor performance.

Some studies find a difference in poor parents' 'stated' and 'revealed' preferences for school selection (Trivitt and Wolf 2011; Thieme and Treviño 2013; Elacqua et al. 2006). Teske and Schneider (2001: 613) believe that 'while there is no doubt that low-income parents at least report making school choices based mainly on academic issues, there is more debate about their actual behaviour.' Even when parents select schools based on race or other non-academic criteria, actual parental selections seem to be related to learning (Hastings and Weinstein 2008).

Parental school selections should be compared with student preferences as students directly experience learning and the school environment. It is possible that poor students align their preferences with learning and school quality faster than their parents. Comparing parental and student reasons for choosing cyber schooling, Beck et al. (2016) find that rural parents are more apt to choose cyber schooling for reasons including a broader range of classes as well as avoiding long commutes to school. On the other hand, the students were more likely to state curricular reasons as their decision to choose cyber schooling.

Field work in developing countries shows that poor parents often reject free government schools and opt for low-cost private schools (Dixon 2013; Tooley 2009), even when private schools may not be recognised by the government. There has been a consistent increase in the share of low-cost private schools in developing countries over time, even after taking into account the increase in the supply of free public schools. Elimination of school fees in Kenya, even though it was praised by international governments and aid agencies, failed to shut down the private school market (Tooley 2009; Tooley et al. 2008). Such private schools were financed through fees paid for by poor families who chose the schools because of their higher perceived quality over the free public schools. Other reasons for choosing private schools in such communities is that the schools have grown organically, the school owner and teachers all living within the slum neighbourhood. International aid is often targeted exclusively to the public school system in developing countries, in at least some cases exacerbating the low quality of the already unpopular public schools (Moyo 2010; Dixon 2013).

Poor parents appear to base their school choices on sound reasons connected with their child's needs. The more involved and experienced poor families are with school choice, the more active they seem to be in their schools and the more accurate information they appear to have about them. The best validation of the ability of poor parents to choose schools would come from evidence that their children and society experience better outcomes as a result. We turn to that matter next.

Evidence on educational outcomes from parental selections

A review of over one hundred empirical studies shows that school choice programmes are associated with improved results for students across a variety of outcomes (Forster 2016). The experimental interventions studying student achievement were largely targeted towards economically disadvantaged families. No overall evidence exists that poor students get harmed by school choice. In fact, experimental evidence shows moderate benefits in achievement over time for students from poor families. More interestingly, when school choice interventions found null effects for economically advantaged groups, statistically significant and positive achievement effects are observed for disadvantaged minorities (Howell et al. 2002).

Opponents of school choice warn that parental preferences for religion and cultural values may lead to increased segregation by race. Swanson (2017) finds that evidence on impacts of choice on racial segregation is context-specific. It is not conclusively established that segregation is exacerbated by school choice. For private school choice, Swanson reports, seven out of eight studies have found positive impacts of choice on racial integration while the remaining study found null effects. Based on the available evidence it seems private schooling is the best school choice option to integrate students in the US. Moreover, research on segregation as a consequence of school choice often fails to adjust for segregation occurring as a consequence of neighbourhood assignment due to public schools.

Private schools are better able to cater to religious and cultural sentiments of poor families than public schools. A systematic review of the effect of private schools in developing countries (Ashley and Wales 2015: 5) notes that:

> In terms of supply, a common finding is that private and philanthropic schools (with little evidence on religious schools) fare better in terms of quality learning outcomes (moderate evidence) and teaching (strong evidence) compared with state schools.

In India, knowledge of the English language is seen as a market signal for quality schooling by poor parents (Mitra et al. 2003; Tooley and Dixon 2002). Experimental evidence on school vouchers in India shows a positive impact on English language learning for poor students (Wolf et al. 2015).

Evidence from quasi-experimental and experimental evaluations of private schools show that private schools outperform public schools in the US on civic value outcomes (DeAngelis 2017; Wolf 2007). Using data from the 1999 and 2009 rounds of the International Association for the Evaluation of Educational Achievement's civic education study, school choice is found to be associated with improved civic attitudes of students in Sweden (Shafiq and Myers 2014). This is especially interesting as another study found a moderate increase in school segregation in Sweden fifteen years after 1992, when a universal school voucher reform was introduced (Böhlmark et al. 2015). If students' civic attitudes improve as a result of school choice when slight increases in school segregation take place, school choice might contribute to the overall social good. This possibility should be considered empirically by researchers who study segregation resulting from school choice, as integration should be merely a means to the more important end of strong civic values.

Rigorous experimental evidence for targeted school voucher and Charter School interventions shows that both private schools and Charter Schools produce moderately better student test scores than public schools over time (Shakeel et al. 2016; Betts and Tang 2014). School voucher interventions are generally cost-effective as they produce equal or slightly better outcomes than public schools over time, at a lower cost per student (Shakeel et al. 2017). Charter Schools are also generally more productive than traditional public schools as they deliver a higher return on investment (Wolf et al. 2014).

In some developing countries, there is a large achievement gap by gender. Experimental studies in India and Pakistan have found increases in girls' enrolment and achievement as a consequence of private school choice (Wolf et al. 2015; Muralidharan and Sundararaman 2015; Kim et al. 1999). Two voucher programmes in Pakistan and Colombia were focused on the countries' poorest groups. Both programmes were found to improve equity by increasing private school enrolment among the poor (Morgan et al. 2015).

Most research that focuses on evaluation of school choice programmes uses student achievement as the primary outcome measure. Yet long-term outcomes involving education attainment, such as high school completion, college enrolment and college persistence may be of larger relevance as they are closely tied to the well-being and earnings of an individual. A review of public and private school choice studies in the US shows a positive association between school choice and the educational attainment of participants (Foreman 2017).

Using more than 150 statistical comparisons covering eight different educational outcomes, Coulson (2009) found that private schools outperformed government schools in the majority of studies across the globe. Hence, experimental, quasi-experimental, descriptive and qualitative evidence shows that school choice helps the disadvantaged. It is not empirically established that school choice harms the poor, especially when we look at educational outcomes based on rigorous experimental evidence.

Conclusion and policy implications

It is a myth that poor families do not have choice, cannot make sound school choices or are harmed by doing so. Overall, empirical evidence shows that generally poor parents are active choosers and willingly participate in choice programmes. School choice creates incentives for the more-disadvantaged and less-informed parent to engage in the education of their children. Thus they can then align their experiences with their children's learning. Both econometric and qualitative evidence exists for looking at school choice from the perspective of family empowerment

(Shakeel et al. 2017; Stewart and Wolf 2016). When quality free education options are lacking in developing countries, poor parents create choice without the support of the state. No comprehensive evidence exists that school choice harms the poor when we look at educational outcomes such as achievement, attainment, college completion or civic values.

Gintis (1995) argues that the poverty of individuals is proportional to the barriers they face in exercising real choice, because of a shortage of quality information or a lack of skills to interpret the information that is available. The evidence does not universally support this jaundiced view of the capacity of poor parents to be school choosers, especially given the frequency of school choice activities by families living in abject poverty in developing countries. It is also premature to evaluate a poor family's choice options based on early years of transferring to a new school of choice or by evaluating choice based solely on test scores. The latest results from a state-wide voucher programme in Louisiana shows that test scores improve with time after an initial dip (Mills and Wolf 2017b).

When evaluating school choice, such parental concerns as student safety and cultural sensitivities should also be taken into consideration. School choice saves money by generally producing equal or better educational outcomes at substantially lower per-student cost than public schools. It is not conclusively established that school choice leads to segregation, and the evidence is context-specific. More interestingly, it is possible that in cases of moderate segregation students' civic values nevertheless improve. Hence, segregation should be differentiated from stratification based on voluntary association such as children experience from school choice.

There are some areas where school choice for poor families can be strengthened. First among them is for the government to allow easy access to funds for poor families to educate their children. Education Savings Accounts are seen as the latest promising idea in this direction as they allow families to customise their child's education by spending the funds on a variety of educational products (Butcher and Burke 2016). Second, governments can affect the supply side of school choice by making it easier for new quality schools to start up and by easing the regulations on schools participating in choice programmes (Sude et al. 2017). The existence of unrecognised and unaided private schools in the slums of India and parts of Africa show that poor families do not necessarily see government recognition as beneficial in educating their children (Dixon 2013). Third, there is a dearth of experimental as well as rigorous qualitative studies on school choice outside the US. More governments may benefit from limited school choice experiments that can bring evidence to bear on the question of whether or not they should scale up school choice programmes to benefit poor parents who, by this review of the evidence, appear to be fully capable school choosers.

References

Abdulkadiroglu, A., Pathak, P. A., Schellenberg, J. and Walters, C. R. (2017) Do parents value school effectiveness? NBER Working Paper 23912.

Angrist, J., Bettinger, E., Bloom, E., King, E. and Kremer, M. (2002) Vouchers for private schooling in Columbia: evidence from a randomized natural experiment. *American Economic Review* 92(5): 1535–58.

Ashley, D. L. and Wales, J. (2015) The impact of non-state schools in developing countries: a synthesis of the evidence from two rigorous reviews. EPPI-Centre, SSRU, UCL Institute of Education, London, UK [DFID Education Rigorous Literature Review].

Beck, D., Maranto, R. and Shakeel, M. D. (2016) Does rural differ? Comparing parent and student reasons for choosing cyber schooling. *The Rural Educator* 37(3): 1–16.

Berner, A. R. (2017) *Pluralism and American Public Education: No One Way to School*. New York: Palgrave/Macmillan.

Betts, J. and Tang, E. (2014) A meta-analysis of the literature on the effect of Charter Schools on student achievement (http://www.crpe.org/sites/default/files/CRPE_meta-analysis_charter-schoolseffect-student-achievement_workingpaper.pdf).

Böhlmark, A., Holmlund, H. and Lindahl, M. (2015) School choice and segregation: evidence from Sweden. Working Paper 2015: 8), IFAU-Institute for Evaluation of Labour Market and Education Policy.

Butcher, J. and Burke, L. M. (2016) The education debit card. II. What Arizona parents purchase with education savings accounts. Friedman Foundation for Education Choice (https://www.edchoice.org/research/the-education-debit-card-ii/).

Chaudhury, N., Hammer, J., Kremer, M., Muralidharan, K. and Rogers, F. H. (2006) Missing in action: teacher and health worker absence in developing countries. *Journal of Economic Perspectives* 20(1): 91–116.

Chubb, J. E. and Moe, T. M. (2011) *Politics, Markets, and America's Schools*. Washington, DC: Brookings Institution Press.

Coulson, A. J. (2009) Comparing public, private, and market schools: the international evidence. *Journal of School Choice* 3(1): 31–54.

Cowen, J. M., Fleming, D. J., Witte, J. F. and Wolf, P. J. (2012) Going public: who leaves a large, longstanding, and widely available urban voucher program? *American Educational Research Journal* 49(2): 231–56.

DeAngelis, C. A. (2017) Do self-interested schooling selections improve society? A review of the evidence. *Journal of School Choice* 11(4): 546–58.

Dixon, P. (2013) *International Aid and Private Schools for the Poor: Smiles, Miracles and Markets*. Cheltenham: Edward Elgar Publishing.

Dixon, P. and Humble, S. (2017) How school choice is framed by parental preferences and family characteristics: a study of Western Area, Sierra Leone. *Journal of School Choice* 11(1): 95–110.

Dixon, P., Humble, S. and Tooley, J. (2017) How school choice is framed by parental preferences and family characteristics: a study in poor areas of Lagos State, Nigeria. *Economic Affairs*, 37(1): 53–65.

Dronkers, J. (2016) Islamic primary schooling in the Netherlands. *Journal of School Choice* 10(1): 6–21.

Dynarski, M., Rui, N., Webber, A., Gutmann, B. and Bachman, M. (2017) Evaluation of the DC Opportunity Scholarship Program: impacts after one year. NCEE 2017-4022, Institute of Education Sciences, National Center for Education Evaluation and Regional Assistance, US Department of Education.

EdChoice (2017) *The ABCs of School Choice, 2017 Edition*. Indianapolis: EdChoice.

Elacqua, G., Gobierno, E. and Ibanez, U. (2004) *School Choice in Chile: An Analysis of Parental Preferences and Search Behaviour*. Santiago: Universidad Adolfo Ibáñez.

Elacqua, G., Schneider, M. and Buckley, J. (2006) School choice in Chile: is it class or the classroom? *Journal of Policy Analysis and Management* 25(3): 577–601.

Farkas, S. and Johnson, J. (1998) Time to move on: African-American and white parents set an agenda for public schools. Public Agenda, 6 East 39th Street, New York.

Foreman, L. M. (2017) Educational attainment effects of public and private school choice. *Journal of School Choice* 11(4): 642–54.

Forster, G. (2016) *A Win–Win Solution: The Empirical Evidence on School Choice*. Indianapolis: Friedman Foundation.

Fuller, B. F. and Elmore, R. (1996) *Who Chooses? Who Loses? Culture, Institutions and the Unequal Effects of School Choice*. New York: Teachers College Press.

Gintis, H. (1995) The political economy of school choice. *Teachers College Record* 96: 492–511.

Glenn, C. L. and Candal, C. S. (2012) *Balancing Freedom, Autonomy, and Accountability in Education* (ed. Charles L. Glenn and J. De Groof). Wolf Legal Publishers (WLP).

Hamilton, L. S. and Guin, K. (2005) Understanding how families choose schools. In *Getting Choice Right: Ensuring Equity and Efficiency in Education Policy* (ed. J. R. Betts and T. Loveless). Washington, DC: Brookings Institution Press.

Hanuchek, E. A., Kain, J. F. and Rivkin, S. G. (2004) Disruption versus Tiebout improvement: the costs and benefits of switching schools. *Journal of Public Economics* 88(9–10): 1721–46.

Hastings, J. S. and Weinstein, J. M. (2008) Information, school choice, and academic achievement: evidence from two experiments. *Quarterly Journal of Economics* 123(4): 1373–414.

Howell, W. G. and Peterson, P. E. (2006). *The Education Gap: Vouchers and Urban Schools.* Brookings Institution Press.

Howell, W. G., Wolf, P. J., Campbell, D. E. and Peterson, P. E. (2002) School vouchers and academic performance: results from three randomized field trials. *Journal of Policy Analysis and Management* 21(2): 191–217.

Humble, S. and Dixon, P. (2017) School choice, gender and household characteristics: evidence from a household survey in a poor area of Monrovia, Liberia. *International Journal of Educational Research* 84: 13–23.

Kim, J., Alderman, H. and Orazem, P. F. (1999) Can private school subsidies increase enrollment for the poor? The Quetta Urban Fellowship Program. *The World Bank Economic Review* 13(3): 443–65.

Kisida, B. and Wolf, P. J. (2010) School governance and information: does choice lead to better-informed parents? *American Politics Research* 38(5): 783–805.

Lovenheim, M. F. and Walsh, P. (2017) Does choice increase information? Evidence from online school search behavior. No. w23445. National Bureau of Economic Research.

Martinez, V. J., Godwin, R. K., Kemerer, F. R. and Perna, L. (1995) The consequences of school choice: who leaves and who stays in the inner city. *Social Science Quarterly*, pp. 485–501.

Mills, J. N. and Wolf, P. J. (2017a) Vouchers in the bayou: the effects of the Louisiana scholarship program on student achievement after two years *Education Evaluation and Policy Analysis,* 20(10): 1–21.

Mills, J. N. and Wolf, P. J. (2017b) The effects of the Louisiana Scholarship Program on student achievement after three years (Louisiana Scholarship Program Evaluation Report #5). New Orleans, Louisiana: Education Research Alliance for New Orleans & School Choice Demonstration Project, Department of Education Reform, University of Arkansas.

Mitra, S., Tooley, J., Inamdar, P. and Dixon, P. (2003) Improving English pronunciation: an automated instructional approach. *Information Technologies and International Development* 1(1): 75–84.

Mizala, A. and Romaguera, P. (2000) School performance and choice: the Chilean experience. *Journal of Human Resources* 35(2): 392–417.

Morgan, C., Petrosino, A. and Fronius, T. (2015) The impact of school vouchers in developing countries: a systematic review. *International Journal of Educational Research* 72: 70–79.

Moyo, D. (2010) *Dead Aid: Why Aid Makes Things Worse and How There Is Another Way for Africa.* London: Penguin.

Muralidharan, K. and Sundararaman, V. (2015) The aggregate effect of school choice: evidence from a two-stage experiment in India. *Quarterly Journal of Economics* 130(3): 1011–66.

Peterson, P. and Campbell, D. (2001) An evaluation of the Children's Scholarship Fund. John F. Kennedy School of Government Harvard University Faculty Research Working Papers Series. Working Paper 01-03. Program on Education Policy and Governance, Harvard University, Cambridge, MA.

Schneider, M., Teske, P., Marshall, M. and Roch, C. (1998) Shopping for schools: in the land of the blind, the one-eyed parent may be enough. *American Journal of Political Science*, pp. 769–93.

Shafiq, M. N. and Myers, J. P. (2014) Educational vouchers and social cohesion: a statistical analysis of student civic attitudes in Sweden, 1999–2009. *American Journal of Education* 121(1): 111–36.

Shakeel, M. D., Anderson, K. P. and Wolf, P. J. (2016) The participant effects of private school vouchers across the globe: a meta-analytic and systematic review (EDRE Working Paper 2016-07) (https://ssrn.com/abstract=2777633).

Shakeel, M. D., Anderson, K. P. and Wolf, P. J. (2017) The juice is worth the squeeze: a cost-effectiveness analysis of the experimental evidence on private school vouchers across the globe. Paper presented at the *Association for Public Policy Analysis & Management International Conference,* Brussels, Belgium, 13–14 July.

Shakeel, M. D. and DeAngelis, C. A. (2017) Are public schools prison? A comparison of school climate and safety from private and public school principals. Paper presented at the *2017 Annual Conference of the Association of Private Enterprise Education*, 9–12 April, Lahaina, Hawaii.

Stewart, T. and Wolf, P. (2016) *The School Choice Journey: School Vouchers and the Empowerment of Urban Families.* Springer.

Stewart, T., Lucas-McLean, J., Jensen, L. I., Fetzko, C., Ho, B. and Segovia, S. (2010). Family voices on parental school choice in Milwaukee: what can we learn from low-income families? SCDP Milwaukee Evaluation Report #19, School Choice Demonstration Project, University of Arkansas.

Sude, Y., DeAngelis, C. A. and Wolf, P. J. (2017) *Supplying Choice: An Analysis of School Participation Decisions in Voucher Programs in DC, Indiana and Louisiana.* New Orleans: Education Research Alliance.

Swanson, E. (2017) Can we have it all? A review of the impacts of school choice on racial integration. *Journal of School Choice.* 11(4): 507–26.

Teske, P. and Schneider, M. (2001) What research can tell policymakers about school choice. *Journal of Policy Analysis and Management* 20(4): 609–31.

Thieme, C. and Treviño, E. (2013) School choice and market imperfections: evidence from Chile. *Education and Urban Society* 45(6): 635–57.

Tooley, J. (2009) *The Beautiful Tree: A Personal Journey into How the World's Poorest People Are Educating Themselves.* New Delhi: Penguin.

Tooley, J. (2012) *From Village School to Global Brand: Changing the World through Education.* London: Profile Books.

Tooley, J. and Dixon, P. (2002) *Private Schools for the Poor: A Case Study from India.* Reading, UK: Centre for British Teachers.

Tooley, J., Dixon, P. and Stanfield, J. (2008) Impact of free primary education in Kenya: a case study of private schools in Kibera. *Educational Management, Administration and Leaderships* 36(4): 449–69.

Trivitt, J. R. and Wolf, P. J. (2011) School choice and the branding of Catholic schools. *Education Finance and Policy* 6(2): 202–45.

Witte, J. F. (2000) *The Market Approach to Education: An Analysis of America's First Voucher Program.* Princeton University Press.

Wolf, P. J. (2007) Civics exam. *Education Next* 7(3): 66–72.

Wolf, P. J., Cheng, A., Batdorff, M., Maloney, L., May, J. and Speakman, S. (2014) The productivity of Charter Schools. The School Choice Demonstration Project, Department of Education Reform, University of Arkansas, Fayetteville.

Wolf, P. J., Egalite, A. J. and Dixon, P. (2015) Private school choice in developing countries: experimental results from Delhi, India. In *Handbook of International Development and Education* (ed. P. Dixon, S. Humble and C. Counihan), pp. 456–71. Cheltenham: Edward Elgar.

Wolf, P. J. and Macedo, S. (eds) (2004) *Educating Citizens: International Perspectives on Civic Values and School Choice*. Brookings Institution Press.

Zhang, A., Musu-Gillette, L. and Oudekerk, B. A. (2016) Indicators of school crime and safety: 2015. NCES 2016-079. NCJ 249758. National Center for Education Statistics.

8 CHOOSING EDUCATION: EVIDENCE FROM INDIA AND TOWARDS A TRANSACTIONAL ECOLOGICAL APPROACH

Chris Counihan

Introduction

As policymakers, experts and laypeople debate the effectiveness of school choice in the West in finding quality education for all, parents all over India have already taken control. In this chapter, I present evidence of an emerging grassroots educational phenomenon gripping one of the world's most extensive education systems. Encouragingly, where systematic state intervention has failed the poorest of Indian society, a new system driven by parental choice is emerging. Through the application of caveat emptor principles, poor parents are seen as active choosers of schools and take responsibility for the decisions they make. While there is limited literature on school choice operating in the developing world, there is a nascent shift towards understanding 'choice' as an active option for poor parents. These implications are discussed, paying particular reference to the shape of poor parents' school choice via a transactional ecological framework.

The chapter is organised in the following way. Firstly, recent reforms and challenges facing the Indian education system are investigated to give a general overview. From here, there is a focus on an emerging area of parental choice and how this can be realised by supporting an independent approach. This is supplemented by identifying essential studies that have looked at education vouchers and their effectiveness in promoting school choice. The final section presents some policy recommendations and suggestions for the way forward.

Education unleashed

We might think of school choice in India as a recent phenomenon, but parents have been choosing educational providers for centuries. Before the British arrived in India, a thriving indigenous private system of education was commonplace and reached the most impoverished states and regions of India's core heartland (Dixon 2013; Tooley 2009). The commentary on the schools of yesteryear paints an interesting narrative of availability, scale and quality (Tooley 2009). School choice enabled social connections and literate populations. Some of the pedagogical tools developed in India such as the Madras Method were also adopted in schools throughout Victorian England (Counihan 2015). However, as in much of the developed world, a stampede of imperialist ideas of mass state educational infrastructure and administration followed and eroded an already fully functioning system. As Mahatma Gandhi, speaking at London's Chatham House in 1931, explained (cited in Dharampal 1995: 6):

> I defy anybody to fulfil a programme of compulsory primary education of these masses inside of a century. This very poor country of mine is ill able to sustain such an expensive method of education.

Of course, he was right. The shift from indigenous methods to a completely alien system did no favours for his people at the time. Indeed, the legacy of this can be found in much of India's state provision more recently. There has been progress since then, but you have to wonder what might have been.

The economic liberalisation of the Indian economy in 1991, overseen by the then former prime minister, Narasimha Roa, and his chief finance minister, Manmohan Singh, led to the end of the 'Licence Raj' and a shift towards a free market economy. The change in economic policy led to new markets and a redefinition of the burgeoning middle class. New hopes and aspirations were placed on sectors to redesign provision and fulfil what society craved: mass education for all. It eventually led to a repositioning of how education interacted with poor families and raised questions of equity and how state systems provided it. Moreover, studies of the time debunked government policies and perceptions of parental apathy towards education: that parents in rural areas preferred sending their children to labour in fields rather than classrooms (Vaidyanathan and Nair 2001).

As a consequence of the new regulations, aspirations among the poor changed – driven by educational opportunity and social and economic mobility. In recent times, this drive has coincided with the proliferation of the low-cost schooling market. These schools are fee-paying enterprises that offer educational services at an affordable cost. They are a popular option for some of India's poorest families and there are thought to be around 400,000 of them (Garg 2011, cited in Tooley 2015: 23). Given their ubiquity, it is essential to understand why parents choose this option, given that the state option is free, and in some cases offers incentives (Dixon 2013) to go to school – such as midday meals and uniforms. Mostly, the literature is concentrated around a perceived lack of quality (Tooley et al. 2008) and a lack of state schooling options in localities (Heyneman and Stern 2014). How does this impact parental choice? Literature from an Indian (or even international development) perspective is limited, but there are some shifts towards understanding choice at the household level, and this is the focus of the next section.

Towards a parental choice ecology

With the proliferation of low-cost private schools in India, critics have raised questions about whether they offer a real option for poorer families. Some of these arguments focus on equity issues such as gender preferences/disparities (Azam and Kingdon 2013), the economic climate of households (Härmä 2011) and caste type (Woodhead et al. 2013). Whatever your position on the low-fee option, it is foolish not to notice the spreading of these schools throughout the country; it is, after all, parents selecting this opportunity that is central to their ubiquity. You only have to look at recent trends from Kingdon (2017: 14), who analysed data between 2010 and 2014 and found private school enrolment rose by 16 million compared to state school enrolment, which fell by 11.1 million students. This grassroots revolution is indicative of parents taking control of their children's education destinies, and not waiting for mass government planning or intervention.

There is good support for choice (Day Ashley et al. 2014) but most would agree there is a need to know more about how parents make their choices. Are parents reliably informed? Or are they making unconscious decisions about schools? To answer these crucial questions, we must locate the school choice movement as an essential process. In particular, we need to define 'family' and the type of society it sits within. We can do this by following an ecological transactional approach (Sameroff 2009) to get a better understanding of the interplay between educational environments and factors that influence choice. The process is not unidirectional but reciprocated at every interconnected level. In this way, just as parents' culture, beliefs and values influence how schools are chosen, the chosen schools may influence how culture, beliefs and values of parents are constructed (MacKenzie and McDonough 2009).

As James and Woodhead (2014) note, school choice factors are not simple and are perceived differently from one household to the next. Specifically, they point to the availability of schools, perceived quality inputs and cost implications as proxies for decisions made on education destinations.

To understand this better, recent research has started to emerge on the types of decision made at the household level. For example, Srivastava's (2008) study investigated parents' decisions on schooling by investigating choice in one rural and one urban school. The study included 60 interviews of low-income parents and reported the underlying choices they made. It found that parents are very much 'active choosers' when it comes to making decisions on school selection. More interestingly, it cites their ability to differentiate between macro and micro policies and procedures dominating the national and local landscapes. Following transactional principles, poor parents are selecting proximal services in spite of distal influences such as socioeconomic status and education policies that typically influence choice behaviour. In Srivastava's study, at the macro level, parents exercised their awareness of national agendas and policies by reporting their frustration and anger towards aspects of state-provided education arrangements, such as regular teacher absenteeism, general attitudes towards teaching activities and facilities/infrastructure.

Research into these areas agrees with the parents. for example, Kremer and Muralidharan (2008) reported teacher absenteeism higher in state schools than in private schools. On teaching and learning, Singh (2013) found teachers located in rural private providers took a flexible approach to their teaching style, adapting it to the needs of students. These approaches were found to be positively linked to achievement outcomes. Indeed, the evidence of consistent teacher–student contact time is more prevalent with low-cost private providers than it is in state education (Tooley et al. 2011, Maitra et al. 2011). Srivastrava's (2008) study reports a preference for private schools but goes further to understand why parents view private provision as superior, their general attitudes and more importantly how they judge quality among providers. It is perhaps one of the first studies to dispel the myth that parents are incapable of choosing their child's schooling.

More recently, another study by Gurney (2017) found a deeper understanding of choice that is related to parents' own stories, expectations and life transitions. Broadly, some parents from the sample recognised schooling choices as an important feature of being a good parent. Pressures from others selecting schools challenged their own beliefs of what constitutes a good education. Others stated that their own educational experiences, which for most mothers was limited to a few years of primary schooling, was what inspired their passion for selecting schools. Indeed, the study supplies quotes from parents based on their own time in state schools, it includes such responses (ibid.: 28) as 'we know exactly what happens there ... no-one is concerned about kids' education' and 'I have a dream that while I have studied in a government school, my children should go to a private school'.

Wanting to provide a better education for your children isn't new: just about every parent on the planet buys into this idea. However, parents citing their personal experience of state failure helps to build a picture as to why school choice is enthusiastically exercised throughout India. The finding corroborates with Srivastrava's (2008) previous findings on state schooling failures and frustrations among parents.

Vouchers and choices

Only recently have Friedman's (1962) ideas of minimal state intervention in education attracted attention in developing-world contexts. Building on his ideas that parents could access educational services through targeted vouchers is a relatively new policy area for some developing countries, unlike the extensive political debate and research in his native America. Using vouchers, a parent would select a school operating in a market of schooling providers. The benefits of this approach allow parents to judge for themselves the type of school they want their child to attend and hold it accountable, thus creating competition among providers to ensure quality benchmarks and standards meet the demand side (Dixon 2013). Should schools not perform, parents would leave and select another provider. It is therefore of significant importance that schools co-develop partnerships in their educational offer to ensure quality happens and parents are supported. The central idea permits choice as a pillar of liberal civility and is an excellent example of democracy-in-action (Levin 1991). Some studies have emerged with varying results on the overall effectiveness of learning and achievement, this already reflecting the patterns found in the West. However, it is crucial to view findings in context, and it is here where we start with the latest results from a voucher experiment in India's Andhra Pradesh.

The study conducted by Muralidharan and Sundararaman (2015) is influential with both critics and supporters of parental choice. Through adopting an experimental randomised control trial (RCT) design, it stands as the first study to measure the impact of a school choice programme and its effectiveness in a developing-world context. Their programme ran for four years and included a large sample population, from five Districts of rural Andhra Pradesh, which accounted for 23 per cent of students enrolled in government schools who shifted to private providers in the preselected voucher villages. The study included baseline and post-tests (typical for RCT designs) in a number of cognitive tasks namely: English, maths and Telegu (the state medium of instruction). These tests were administered in the second and fourth years, while tests in Hindi (one of India's three constitutional national languages), science and environmental science were administered in year four.

The general findings from the programme suggested children receiving vouchers were not statistically significantly different to non-voucher children on each of the tests apart from Hindi, which in this context is mainly taught in private schools and not in state schools, thus rendering the difference unsurprising. Overall, private schools compared to state provision show no difference in achievement. However, perusal of costs per student reveal that 'the annual cost per student in the public school system is more than three times the mean cost per student in the private schools' (ibid.: 1014–15). From an accountability measure, you would be forgiven for asking why state schools cost more per student but offer no extra value? However, critics of vouchers would hone in on the achievement factor. For example, Karopady (2014) questions the performance of private schools for not adding value. However, the reality in this study is that government schools are costing more than three times the private school equivalent but are not outperforming them. This raises important questions about the financing of state schools and their effectiveness in driving up achievement and quality. Before we take pessimistic or optimistic stances, we need more detail about the study's methodology and other findings.

Starting with the former: typically, RCTs are designed in such a way that all study participants are allocated to either a control or intervention group through randomised processes; the study population must be similar to allow for greater power in interpreting the final results (Hutchinson and Styles 2010). The only difference will be the treatment groups (in this case those children receiving a voucher) will be different from the control group (those who were not successful in gaining a voucher). So far, so good, for the study's methodology. However, the difficulties begin when we learn that the tests administered to the control and intervention groups were not the same. Tests were conducted in two different languages – Telegu for children tested in state schools and English for children in private schools (Tooley 2016). One of the assumptions about low-cost private schools is that they teach almost exclusively in English. However, there tends to be a graduated transition from native language(s) in the early primary years to English in the middle primary to high school (Karopady 2014). This would mean that the results were not (by RCT standards) robust enough to show fundamental differences – tests were not the same because they were administered in different languages. Children in private schools would be disadvantaged based on language limitations, and this reduces the reliability of the findings. As a direct reply to the study by Muralidharan and Sundararaman (2015), a detailed explanation is provided by Tooley (2016), who illustrates these difficulties for children from lower grades switching from a native language to English in a test scenario. Conversely, all is not lost. The second half of the study introduced aggregated measures where half of the study population received the same tests (conducted in the same language) and this time found statistically significant differences where private schools outperformed state schools. The finding is significant for school choice activists but, more importantly, for understanding the complexities of designing trials in a developing-world context.

Other voucher studies employing similar designs have found positive results in favour of choice. An RCT study by Dixon et al. (2015), managed by the global charity Absolute Return for Kids (ARK), found encouraging results for learning effectiveness. The programme ran over two years and reported statistically significant gains in English for voucher children compared with non-voucher holders. Moreover, it shows statistically significant positive outcomes for voucher-winning girls in Hindi, maths and English, compared with non-voucher holders. Girls who were awarded vouchers even outperformed their male voucher counterparts. This is encouraging news for school choice proponents but also a positive step in opening up options for girls, this being an area of growing importance in international policy and development agendas.

The Centre for Civil Society (CCS) oversaw another programme operating in Delhi. CCS claims to have launched the first voucher programme in India (CMS Social 2009). The results are fascinating. Working in 68 wards across Delhi, they employed a mixed-method RCT following a quasi-experimental design, in which 408 children were awarded educational vouchers through a lottery process; winners were funded up to RS3,600 per annum, over a three-year period. Following RCT principles, the programme aimed to compare voucher-winning children against two control groups: (a) children from the same school grade but who were unsuccessful in gaining a voucher and (b) children from district state schools and pre-schools who were also unsuccessful in receiving a voucher from the original lottery. Both of these groups recruited 371 children to take part. All children were tested in English, maths and Hindi and were compared to voucher-winning children's performance at the end of the first year.

The main finding of the study at the end of year one was that voucher-winning children outperformed non-voucher children in private and state schools in English, maths and Hindi. It is further evidence that parents can select appropriate schools for their children, whether private or state. Alongside the tests, researchers also interviewed voucher-winning parents to learn more about their school choice preferences and habits after receiving the voucher. The study found that 63 per cent of parents of voucher-winning children shifted from state provision to low-cost private schools, and reported a fear of funding not continuing after the programme. This suggests that parents were happy with their initial choice and were worried about placing their children back in government schools. Further evidence from the parental interviews revealed that over 90 per cent were happy with their child's learning, teachers and discipline.

Taken altogether, there is emerging evidence from research to suggest poor parents are actively involved in the school choice process. This active process isn't confined to one-off situations but is rather a reaction to failing state services. The dynamic transactions parents make based on their proximal and distal connections to education are less known. Future research will confirm parental aspiration, but whether a choice is fully informed or not, we must banish the myth that the poor cannot choose what is right for their children,

Policy recommendations and emergent quality factors

We can all agree on the macro ideas of what education quality involves – having good teachers, schools and opportunities in every village, township or city. The problem is *how* we agree on these critical ingredients. There is a significant debate about what constitutes 'quality' education and what it looks like at the school level. Indeed, ever since the development agenda orientated towards 'goals-based' solutions, never before has there been such a focus on what quality should look like. However, the quality agenda is governed by ideology and used as a political football. Can we assume 'quality' education to have universal properties? That is, will what works in one country work in another? Consider this concerning locality: what works in the Punjab may not work in the same way in Andhra Pradesh – there are obvious cultural and linguistic variations. There is no absolute standard of what constitutes 'quality' when understanding it as a top-down process. Expert panels cannot agree on its definition; alas, this is where the problems lie.

Instead, we should take a step back and go for bottom-up approaches. Moreover, we should think more about the dynamics of parental transactional ecologies that shape school choice. In this way, we can redefine quality as an emergent area of concentration via empowered individualism. Choice, in this regard, is part of a parent's arsenal. It unleashes a process where 'active choosers' have knowledge and awareness of quality inputs, whatever they may be. To ensure this happens, we must consider creating an education ecosystem that allows parents to choose. Quality inputs from the service side are redesigned and tailored to that of the interested parent, thus allowing for quality to emerge concurrently with student maturation – while leading them towards better learning outcomes and achievement. In this way, quality is measured over a more extended period and will be tailored to the individual. This freedom to develop educational systems in this way is the dream of most start-up schools, but there are obstacles in the way.

Two other factors associated with quality are, firstly, that 'edupreneurs' don't have restrictions facing them when setting up schools, thus allowing them to meet demand by directly responding with targeted supply, and, secondly, that parents have enough information to make effective choices from the range of school types on offer.

On the former, school closures have been rife throughout India (NISA 2017), driven by Section 18 of the Right to Education Act (RTE) 2009, which mandates all private providers to have secured a recognition certificate. It seems a little ironic that this Act, given what it was set up to do, has displaced hundreds of thousands of children as a result of school closures, while simultaneously removing parental rights to select an educational provider. The removal of parental choice has significant implications for general access and achievement. Instead, schools should be allowed to open without restrictions as currently imposed by RTE. One way around this is currently being developed through the Self-Financed Independent School Act (2017) in Andhra Pradesh (Das 2017). The idea is to allow private schools to set up without all the bureaucratic features from local and national bodies. It gives private schools autonomy in setting their fees (without caps) and managing their own admissions policies. Using the Andhra model as a scalable option for other States in India, private schools should consider publishing their school results and teacher qualifications leading them to become more visible in public domains. It would enable parents to make better choices when selecting schools for their children.

Conclusion

This chapter set out to dispel myths surrounding the narrative that poor parents struggle to make rational choices when it comes to selecting schools. In this way, it briefly explored historical and contemporary evidence that has shaped opinions on both sides of the school choice debate. For India, the failure of state provision has allowed for the genesis of a low-cost private school market and for it to thrive and prosper. These schools have reformed from their native beginnings to more rounded schools encompassing modern curricula and offering a viable option for enabling social mobility. It is these innovations, coupled with state failings, that have attracted parents to their provision.

The second part of the chapter looked at the emergence of a parental choice ecology that identifies parents who are actively involved in the school selection process. This is a young field of inquiry but an encouraging one. We now know that parents are making choices (whether informed or through shared discussions) and these lead to positive outcomes for learning and educational transitions. There are enormous opportunities for education providers and the state to support this process by opening up the supply chain through vouchers and other incentives to promote choice.

The simple truth is, parents are not waiting around for government assistance. Instead, they are now offered some options and are tailoring their choices concerning their wants and desires. If Indian educational planners are serious about education for all, they should follow the footprint trail left by parents.

References

Azam, M. and Kingdon, G. G. (2013) Are girls the fairer sex in India? Revisiting intra-household allocation of education expenditure. *World Development* 42: 143–64.

CMS Social (2009) *Delhi Voucher Project: First Assessment Report.* Delhi, India: Centre for Civil Society.

Counihan, C. (2015) Endogenous education in India and the implications of universal peer teaching in the 19th century. In *Handbook of International Development and Education* (ed. P. Dixon, S. Humble and C. Counihan). Cheltenham: Edward Elgar.

Das, G. (2017) Why governments shouldn't mess with private school fees. *Times of India,* 6 August.

Day Ashley, L., Mcloughlin, C., Aslam, M., Engel, J., Wales, J., Rawal, S. and Rose, P. (2014) *The Role and Impact of Private Schools in Developing Countries: A Rigorous Review of the Evidence.* London: Department for International Development.

Dixon, P. (2013) The parting of the veil – low-cost private schools – the evidence. In *International Aid and Private Schools for the Poor: Smiles, Miracles, and Markets* (ed. P. Dixon). Cheltenham: Edward Elgar.

Dixon, P., Wolf, P. and Egalite, A. (2015) Private school choice in developing countries: experimental results from Delhi, India. In *Handbook of International Development and Education* (ed.

P. Dixon, S. Humble and C. Counihan). Cheltenham: Edward Elgar.

Dharampal, W. (1995) *The Beautiful Tree: Indigenous Education in the Eighteenth Century.* Coimbatore: Keerthi Publishing House.

Friedman, M. (1962) *Capitalism and Freedom.* University of Chicago Press

Garg, N. (2011) Low-cost private education in India: challenges and way forward. MIT Sloan School of Management.

Gurney, E. (2017) Choosing schools, choosing selves: exploring the influence of parental identity and biography on the school choice process in Delhi, India. *International Studies in Sociology of Education* 26(1): 19–35.

Härmä, J. (2011) Low-cost private schooling in India: is it pro-poor and equitable? *International Journal of Educational Development* 31(4): 350–56.

Heyneman, S. P. and Stern, J. M. B. (2014) Low-cost private schools for the poor: what public policy is appropriate? *International Journal of Educational Development* 35: 3–15.

Hutchinson, D. and Styles, B. (2010) *A Guide to Running Randomised Controlled Trials for Educational Researchers.* Slough: NFER.

James, Z. and Woodhead, M. (2014) Choosing and changing schools in India's private and government sectors: Young Lives evidence from Andhra Pradesh. *Oxford Review of Education* 40(1): 73–90.

Karopady, D. D. (2014) Does school choice help rural children from disadvantaged sections: evidence from longitudinal research in Andhra Pradesh. *Economic and Political Weekly* XLIX (51): 46–52.

Kingdon, G. (2017) The emptying of public schools and growth of private schools in India. In *Report on Budget Private Schools in India 2017*. Delhi, India: Centre for Civil Society.

Kremer, M. and Muralidharan, K. (2008) Public and private schools in rural India. In *School Choice International* (ed. P. Peterson and R. Chakrabarti). Cambridge, MA: MIT Press.

Levin, H. (1991) The economics of educational choice. *Economics of Education Review* 10: 137–58.

MacKenzie, M. J. and McDonough, S. C. (2009). Transactions between perception and reality: maternal beliefs and infant regulatory behavior. In *A Transactional Model of Development: How Children and Contexts Shape Each Other* (ed. A. J. Sameroff). Washington, DC: American Psychological Association.

Maitra, P., Pal, S. and Sharma, A. (2011) *Reforms, Growth and Persistence of Gender Gap: Recent Evidence from Private School Enrolment in India*. Bonn: Institute for the Study of Labor.

Muralidharan, K. and Sundararaman, V. (2015) The aggregate effect of school choice: evidence from a two-stage experiment in India. *Quarterly Journal of Economics* 130: 1011–66.

National Independent Schools Alliance (NISA) (2017) Data on school closures due to RTE Act (http://nisaindia.org/data-on -school-closures).

Sameroff, A. J. (2009) The transactional model. In *A Transactional Model of Development: How Children and Contexts Shape Each Other* (ed. A. J. Sameroff). Washington, DC: American Psychological Association.

Singh, A. (2013) Size and sources of private school premium in India. Young Lives Working Paper 98, Oxford.

Srivastava, P. (2008) School choice in India: disadvantaged groups and low-fee private schools. In *The Globalisation of*

School Choice? Oxford Studies in Comparative Education (ed. M. Forsey, S. Davies and G. Walford). Oxford: Symposium Books.

Tooley, J. (2009) *The Beautiful Tree: A Personal Journey into How the World's Poorest People Are Educating Themselves.* New Delhi: Penguin.

Tooley J. (2015) Low cost private schools: controversy and implications concerning EFA debate. *ZEP (Zeitschrift für Internationale Bildungsforschung und Entwicklungspädagogik)* 38(2): 22–26.

Tooley, J. (2016) Extending access to low-cost private school through vouchers: an alternative interpretation of a two-stage 'School Choice' experiment in India. *Oxford Review of Education* 42(5): 579–93.

Tooley, J., Dixon, P. and Stanfield, J. (2008) Impact of free primary education in Kenya: a case study of private schools in Kibera. *Educational Management Administration and Leadership* 36(4): 449–69.

Tooley, J., Bao, Y., Dixon, P. and Merrifield, J. (2011) School choice and academic performance: some evidence from developing countries. *Journal of School Choice* 5(1): 1–39.

Vaidyanathan, A. and Nair, G. (eds) (2001) *Elementary Education in Rural India: A Grassroots View.* New Delhi: Sage Publications.

Woodhead, M., Frost, M. and James, Z. (2013) Does growth in private schooling contribute to education for all? Evidence from a longitudinal, two-cohort study in Andhra Pradesh, India. *International Journal of Educational Development* 33(1): 65–73.

ABOUT THE IEA

The Institute is a research and educational charity (No. CC 235 351), limited by guarantee. Its mission is to improve understanding of the fundamental institutions of a free society by analysing and expounding the role of markets in solving economic and social problems.

The IEA achieves its mission by:

- a high-quality publishing programme
- conferences, seminars, lectures and other events
- outreach to school and college students
- brokering media introductions and appearances

The IEA, which was established in 1955 by the late Sir Antony Fisher, is an educational charity, not a political organisation. It is independent of any political party or group and does not carry on activities intended to affect support for any political party or candidate in any election or referendum, or at any other time. It is financed by sales of publications, conference fees and voluntary donations.

In addition to its main series of publications, the IEA also publishes (jointly with the University of Buckingham), *Economic Affairs*.

The IEA is aided in its work by a distinguished international Academic Advisory Council and an eminent panel of Honorary Fellows. Together with other academics, they review prospective IEA publications, their comments being passed on anonymously to authors. All IEA papers are therefore subject to the same rigorous independent refereeing process as used by leading academic journals.

IEA publications enjoy widespread classroom use and course adoptions in schools and universities. They are also sold throughout the world and often translated/reprinted.

Since 1974 the IEA has helped to create a worldwide network of 100 similar institutions in over 70 countries. They are all independent but share the IEA's mission.

Views expressed in the IEA's publications are those of the authors, not those of the Institute (which has no corporate view), its Managing Trustees, Academic Advisory Council members or senior staff.

Members of the Institute's Academic Advisory Council, Honorary Fellows, Trustees and Staff are listed on the following page.

The Institute gratefully acknowledges financial support for its publications programme and other work from a generous benefaction by the late Professor Ronald Coase.

Other books recently published by the IEA include:

Federal Britain: The Case for Decentralisation
Philip Booth
Readings in Political Economy 3; ISBN 978-0-255-36713-4; £10.00

Forever Contemporary: The Economics of Ronald Coase
Edited by Cento Veljanovski
Readings in Political Economy 4; ISBN 978-0-255-36710-3; £15.00

Power Cut? How the EU Is Pulling the Plug on Electricity Markets
Carlo Stagnaro
Hobart Paperback 180; ISBN 978-0-255-36716-5; £10.00

Policy Stability and Economic Growth – Lessons from the Great Recession
John B. Taylor
Readings in Political Economy 5; ISBN 978-0-255-36719-6; £7.50

Breaking Up Is Hard To Do: Britain and Europe's Dysfunctional Relationship
Edited by Patrick Minford and J. R. Shackleton
Hobart Paperback 181; ISBN 978-0-255-36722-6; £15.00

In Focus: The Case for Privatising the BBC
Edited by Philip Booth
Hobart Paperback 182; ISBN 978-0-255-36725-7; £12.50

Islamic Foundations of a Free Society
Edited by Nouh El Harmouzi and Linda Whetstone
Hobart Paperback 183; ISBN 978-0-255-36728-8; £12.50

The Economics of International Development: Foreign Aid versus Freedom for the World's Poor
William Easterly
Readings in Political Economy 6; ISBN 978-0-255-36731-8; £7.50

Taxation, Government Spending and Economic Growth
Edited by Philip Booth
Hobart Paperback 184; ISBN 978-0-255-36734-9; £15.00

Universal Healthcare without the NHS: Towards a Patient-Centred Health System
Kristian Niemietz
Hobart Paperback 185; ISBN 978-0-255-36737-0; £10.00

Sea Change: How Markets and Property Rights Could Transform the Fishing Industry
Edited by Richard Wellings
Readings in Political Economy 7; ISBN 978-0-255-36740-0; £10.00

Working to Rule: The Damaging Economics of UK Employment Regulation
J. R. Shackleton
Hobart Paperback 186; ISBN 978-0-255-36743-1; £15.00

Education, War and Peace: The Surprising Success of Private Schools in War-Torn Countries
James Tooley and David Longfield
ISBN 978-0-255-36746-2; £10.00

Killjoys: A Critique of Paternalism
Christopher Snowdon
ISBN 978-0-255-36749-3; £12.50

Financial Stability without Central Banks
George Selgin, Kevin Dowd and Mathieu Bédard
ISBN 978-0-255-36752-3; £10.00

Against the Grain: Insights from an Economic Contrarian
Paul Ormerod
ISBN 978-0-255-36755-4; £15.00

Ayn Rand: An Introduction
Eamonn Butler
ISBN 978-0-255-36764-6; £12.50

Capitalism: An Introduction
Eamonn Butler
ISBN 978-0-255-36758-5; £12.50

Opting Out: Conscience and Cooperation in a Pluralistic Society
David S. Oderberg
ISBN 978-0-255-36761-5; £12.50

Getting the Measure of Money: A Critical Assessment of UK Monetary Indicators
Anthony J. Evans
ISBN 978-0-255-36767-7; £12.50

Socialism: The Failed Idea That Never Dies
Kristian Niemietz
ISBN 978-0-255-36770-7; £17.50

Top Dogs and Fat Cats: The Debate on High Pay
Edited by J. R. Shackleton
ISBN 978-0-255-36773-8; £15.00

Other IEA publications

Comprehensive information on other publications and the wider work of the IEA can be found at www.iea.org.uk. To order any publication please see below.

Personal customers

Orders from personal customers should be directed to the IEA:

Clare Rusbridge
IEA
2 Lord North Street
FREEPOST LON10168
London SW1P 3YZ
Tel: 020 7799 8907. Fax: 020 7799 2137
Email: sales@iea.org.uk

Trade customers

All orders from the book trade should be directed to the IEA's distributor:

NBN International (IEA Orders)
Orders Dept.
NBN International
10 Thornbury Road
Plymouth PL6 7PP
Tel: 01752 202301, Fax: 01752 202333
Email: orders@nbninternational.com

IEA subscriptions

The IEA also offers a subscription service to its publications. For a single annual payment (currently £42.00 in the UK), subscribers receive every monograph the IEA publishes. For more information please contact:

Clare Rusbridge
Subscriptions
IEA
2 Lord North Street
FREEPOST LON10168
London SW1P 3YZ
Tel: 020 7799 8907, Fax: 020 7799 2137
Email: crusbridge@iea.org.uk